T0166783

PARVATI

Goddess of Love

PARVATI

Goddess of Love

Harsha Dehejia

Mapin Publishing Pvt. Ltd.

First published in the United States of America in 1999 by
Grantha Corporation
80 Cliffedgeway, Middletown, NJ 07701
in association with
Mapin Publishing Pvt. Ltd.
Chidambaram, Ahmedabad 380013 India
web-site: www.mapinpub.com

Distributed in North America by
Antique Collectors' Club
Market Street Industrial Park
Wappingers' Falls, NY 12590
Tel: 800-252-5321 • Fax: 914-297-0068
web-site: www.antiquecc.com

Distributed in the United Kingdom & Europe by
Antique Collectors' Club
5 Church Street, Woodbridge
Suffolk IP12 1DS
Tel: 1394-385-501 • Fax: 1394-384-434
email: accvs@aol.com

Text © Harsha Dehejia
Photographs © as listed
Photographs of the author's personal collection by
Richard Garner, Ottawa, Canada

All rights reserved under international copyright
conventions. No part of this book may be reproduced or
utilised in any form or by any means, electronic or
mechanical, including photocopying, recording or by any
information storage and retrieval system without prior
permission in writing from the publishers.

ISBN: 1-890206-14-8 (Grantha)
ISBN: 81-85822-59-x (Mapin)
LC: 98-68332

Edited by Mallika Sarabhai
Designed by Paulomi Shah / Mapin Design Studio
Colour Separations by Reproscan, Mumbai
Printed in Singapore

Captions:

Front Jacket
Shiva and Parvati in a grove
Kangra, 19th century
(see page 86)

Back Jacket
Standing Parvati
Chola bronze, 11th century
Collection: Asia Society, New York
Gift of Mr. and Mrs.
John D. Rockefeller 3rd
(see page 77)

Frontispiece
Shiva, Parvati and Ganesh
Jaipur, 19th century
Collection: Harsha Dehejia

Enclosed within strong borders is this simple
but eloquent depiction of the Shiva family.
Seated on a terrace with the *haveli* in the
background the dominant colours of the
composition are yellow and blue. The large
bolster, the carpet, Ganesha's *dhoti* and the
frill of the awning are painted in a pleasing
yellow while Parvati and the canopy make a
strong impact in red. The light blue of Shiva's
body and his halo are in contrast to the deep
blue of the space outside. Having deposited
the arm rest on the carpet Shiva's left hand is
ready to embrace Parvati and Ganesha while
he looks expectantly at the mother and child.
Demure looking Parvati seems very motherly
as she caresses the baby Ganesha. Nandi
depicted in bare outline completes the
composition. The artist in creating this
beautiful picture pays a tribute to the
motherhood of Parvati.

Contents

6

Prarambh, As We Begin

vagarthaviva sampraktau vagarthapratipattaye
jagataha pitarau vande parvati paremeshvarau

I salute Parvati and Shiva, the parents of the universe
who are together like word and its meaning
to understand speech.

Kalidasa. *Raghuvamsha*

This book is an appreciation not an anthology, a *vandana* not a *shastra*, a portrait of adoration and not an encyclopaedic account of the many manifestations and meanings of Parvati. Painters and potters, poets and playwrights, pundits and philosophers have given us glimpses of her persona. Many are her songs, countless her stories, numerous her names. She is the daughter of the Himalayas and the queen of Madurai. She is the consort of Shiva and the mother of Ganesha. She is the eternal *shakti* and the objectification of all that is beautiful. She is both *tapasvini* and *vimarshini*, *vama* and *ardhanari*. She is the subject of the Puranas and the inspiration for Adishankara and Kalidasa. She is found in Pahadi paintings and is chiselled in Chola bronzes. She is carved in stone in cave sanctuaries and adorns the walls of temples. Devotees in Maharashtra call her Gauri; those in Madurai worship her as Minakshi, poets eulogise her as Girikanya or daughter of the mountain or Saubhagyajanini or mother of prosperity, while the mountain people celebrate her as Nandadevi. Her names may be different but no matter what form she takes she is always the adorable Parvati.

Uma-Maheshvara
10th century, sandstone
Uttar Pradesh
Collection: Los Angeles County Museum of Art
Gift of Harry & Yvonne Lenart

This elaborate relief of Shiva and Parvati is an inset from the junction-wall between the *rangamandapa* and the sanctum of a temple, a site where such images are commonly placed. The Shiva pantheon is depicted here in an iconic manner. Parvati rests on Shiva's left thigh and amorously embraces him with her right hand while she holds a mirror in her other hand. The four-armed Shiva holds a trident in his upper right hand, a lotus in the lower, and a skull staff entwined with a serpent behind Parvati's head. Below their seat rests Nandi the faithful bull. The emaciated sage Bhringi dances in the centre. Ganesha adorns the right of the panel while Skanda, astride his peacock, rests on the left. Guardian figures make up the borders of the relief. The top of the relief is dominated by Shiva's head with a floral halo and with Brahma and Vishnu with devotees on either side. The mood of the couple is one of serenity and strength in their togetherness.

7

My serious introduction to Parvati came during my study of
Kashmir Shaivism. In its rich epistemological discourses Parvati
was conceptualised as the doorway to higher knowledge, not to be
rejected as an illusion but to be affirmed, not to be negated but to
be celebrated, not just instrumental but inherent in that
transcendent experience of bliss. According to Kashmir Shaivites
she is the very being of Shiva.

Even in the celebratory ethos of Kashmir Shaivism epistemology
Parvati is at best a concept, a consciousness that cognises the
world only to reflect it back thereby exalting our state of being.
But the erudite discourses and scholarly arguments of the masters
of Kashmir Shaivism were able to give me only a glimpse of
Parvati and that too as an aesthetic concept. But concepts are
formless. They are like a melody without words, an aroma without
a flower, a *bhakta* without a deity and love without the beloved. In
keeping with the *agamic* tradition I accepted the ultimate as
formless but longed for a form that I could sensually celebrate. I
longed to discover the Parvati in our arts, the real Parvati, the
Parvati that has inspired our poets and potters over the millennia,
the Parvati that is celebrated in our songs and stories, through
stone and paint. And thus it was that I undertook a quest for that
real Parvati.

Very soon I started discovering that real Parvati in our arts: visual,
literary and performing. No sooner did I feel that I had seen all
the Pahadi miniatures, a new painting would appear before my
eyes. After I felt I had seen all the Chola bronzes of Parvati I
would discover one more, more beautiful than the other. And so it
went. I discovered images of Parvati in museums and libraries,
private collections and public temples. I gathered and collected
and admired all these images and was wonderstruck by the many

images of Parvati. I was like a *bhakta* who was collecting *parijataka* flowers for his morning worship. When he had collected all the flowers that he could find a soft wind blew through the tree and there were more flowers to pick.

Parvati richly revealed herself to me in her variegated and splendorous forms and when my mind was elated with a sense of excitement it was Parvati herself who drew my mind back from the form to the formless. It was she who showed me a mirror that she was holding in her hands, as if to say that in seeking a vision of Parvati I obtained *atmadarshan*, a vision of myself. It was at that stage of my quest that I was able to exclaim *"Shivoham!"* I am Shiva.

Harsha Dehejia
October 20, 1998

The Narrative of Parvati

The Indian tradition is rich with goddesses. So varied are her manifestations and names that every village and every scripture, every *Purana* and poet create their own unique image of her. While sometimes she is a consort, at other times she is a fertility goddess; at times she is a benevolent figure yet at others she is horrific and malevolent. The Shaiva tradition is especially replete with a number of goddesses who are associated with Shiva. Of all the consorts of Shiva the one that is artistically and lovingly the most celebrated is Parvati. Unlike Durga and Kali who assume their own independent religious status in the Hindu pantheon and are worshipped and venerated ritually, Parvati engages the greater attention of poets and painters, musicians and dancers. Numerous are her aspects, varied her persona, multiple her attributes and many her names. Of all the mythic beings in the Hindu pantheon she is perhaps the most loved and undoubtedly the most giving of her love. In her we have the true celebration of Hindu womanhood. Of unsurpassed sensual beauty, her endowment is not merely physical but spiritual, not narcissistic but meant as an offering. In her, it can be said that we have the grand personification of the Hindu expression, as well as the concept of beauty.

As a young girl, daughter of the mountain king Parvat and mother Mena, she is demure and charming. As a young woman she grows into unsurpassed grace and elegance and is the embodiment of perfect sensual beauty, a *sundari*. In her

Shiva and Parvati
16th century, Vijayanagara
Collection: Harsha Dehejia

11

This small Vijayanagara bronze meant for a home shrine inherits the Chola tradition but departs from it in both style and format. Shiva and Parvati are seated in mirror image poses on a double inverted lotus, both holding a trident, a battle axe and a mirror. Absent is the embrace of affectionate togetherness, Nandi and Skanda, but in its place there is a divine presence of the god and goddess ready to receive and bless the devotee. The polished rubbed down forehead of the images suggest that it was worshipped with vermilion.

courtship to the reticent Shiva she is the epitome of *tapasya*, penance, and is Parvati *tapasvini*. As Shiva's consort she becomes his *vama* and *ardhangini*. In her affection towards her two sons Ganesha and Kartikeya she is the loving mother. As his constant companion she leads Shiva to perfect knowledge and becomes Parvati *vimarshini*. As a provider to the mendicant Shiva she is Annapoorna. As Minakshi and Gauri she offers herself to the devout Shiva *bhakta*. And in combining all these diverse roles she is Parvati *yogini*.

Three distinct cultural streams can be identified in Indian civilisation and this leads to at least three streams of Parvati's manifestations. There is the Sanskritic, *nigamic* or Aryan stream, classical and restrained in its outlook, which seeks its origins in the *Vedas* and then culminates in the *Puranas*. The Dravidian stream, equally ancient, runs its own course in the Tamil country, displaying its individual and unique characteristics. And then there is the *agamic*, autochthonous, folk or primal stream, pre-historic and primordial, incorporating folk stories and legends, given to regional variations and expressing itself in its own self-assured and spontaneous style. While remaining proudly independent, the three streams borrow from and contribute to each other, enriching and enlivening the tradition.

There is yet another type of Parvati best described as a hybrid. This version borrows from a variety of streams and cults and creates its own unique icon. An example of this is Lajja Gauri. Originating at a tribal or village level as a *gramadevi* and a fertility goddess she later got Sanskritised and received royal patronage, thus acquiring the status of a pan-Indian goddess. She is frequently associated with Shiva and often looked upon as a manifestation of Parvati.

Thus while the manifestations of Parvati are distinctive in each stream, within the ethos of Indian civilisation these diverse manifestations remain organically tied to one another to give us a holistic picture of this goddess of love. The fact that each tradition claims Parvati as its own speaks of the robustness and pluralistic character of the tradition. It also demonstrates how diverse strands of Hindu tradition, influenced by patronage and driven by social and political factors, were held together through a process of assimilation.

Myth and folklore belong to the people and must grow out of their experiences and imagination, their history and geography. Yet there is something primordial and universal about myths, especially in their enjoyment and celebration as narrative. The religious and artistic expressions of myth are not limited to one tradition or community, and can be shared equally by all devotees and aesthetes of Parvati. Within the tradition Parvati does not always remain a monolithic goddess but acquires different forms and often takes on a composite attribute where she combines the features of different consorts of Shiva. In particular, at the folk and popular level, it is common to see Parvati and Durga intermingle into one goddess.

In calling Parvati the goddess of love it is important to survey briefly the tradition of romantic love, its many manifestations and meanings, and then justify the appellation. *Shringara rasa,* the artistic and creative portrayal of romantic love in the Indian tradition, brings first to mind the *Gathasaptasati,* the earliest extant collection of love poetry in the 4th century court of King Hala in Western India. Here *nayikas,* heroines, talk to parrots, give water to weary travellers or are comforted by their *sakhis* when rain clouds gather and their lovers are nowhere to be found.

With this genre of romantic poetry one is ushered into the secular world of courts and nobility, a world where romantic love was not divided into the narrow compartments of the sacred and the profane.

In another part of the Indian civilisation, a couple of centuries later, Tamil poets were creating their vision of romantic love in the richly evocative and equally secular Sangam literature, an example of which is the Tamil classic *Silappadikaram*. It was also a time when Vatsyayan had eulogised the pleasure-seeking urban elite surrounded by courtesans in his *haveli* as the epitome of culture. In this hushed world of romantic poetry we also find Kalidasa who wove his magic into lyrical and sensuous love poetry like *Meghadoota* and other beautiful love poetry like *Rasamanjari*, *Rasikapriya* and *Sat Sai* later transformed into the idyllic miniature paintings of Rajasthan and the Punjab hills. It was a time in the Indian tradition when sensuality was both affirmed and enjoyed and its indulgence defined haute culture. In a couple of centuries, around the 6th century, it was these well worn romantic idioms that were used to express devotional love, of man for god, and Tamil *bhakti* poetry was born.

The Tamil *bhakti* poet took on the persona of the *nayika* and expressed his devotion to god as a lover would his beloved. *Bhakti* and *shringara* were hues of the same colour and in this lay a whole world-view. It was thus that in the 9th century we enter the romantically surcharged and sensually rich world of the dalliance of Krishna and the *gopis* in the *Bhagavat Purana*. Jayadeva, in the 13th century, inherited this romantic ethos and it was in his *Gita Govinda*, the acme of Sanskrit love poetry, that Radha was to emerge triumphant as the romantic heroine. As we share Radha's thrill of *samyoga* and her pathos of *viyoga* through the richly evocative lyrics of Jayadeva we, along with the poet, identify ourselves with her *sakhis* who, like the landscape around them, rejoice in the joyous coming together of the lovers. This was a turning point in the evolution of the romantic sentiment for as the *Gita Govinda* evolved into the religious ecstasy of Bengal Vaishnavism, one entered the world of Chaitanya, where the romantic love of Radha and Krishna inspired *bhakti*, devotion, in the *rasikas*. What began as romantic idioms of love poetry in the Tamil country flowered into a dialogue of devotion in Bengal.

Radha as the prototypical romantic heroine not only leads us through the dynamics of romantic love and its transformation into the world of loving devotion, but also becomes the embodiment of the doctrine of Vaishnavism. Despite this Radha does not acquire the status of a goddess but remains the prototypical romantic heroine celebrated in literature and painting.

Parvati on the other hand, emerges in the Indian tradition as the true goddess of love. She displays the sentiment of romantic love with finesse. Her dalliance with Shiva in Kailasa has inspired poets and painters alike. Parvati's love affirms romance in all its aspects but then, importantly, surpasses it. In loving Parvati, Shiva discovers the world of *namarupa*, the objective world of name and form, and having cognised this world eventually discovers himself. The *rasa* of *shringara* has now been transformed into the emotion of *adbhuta*, amazement. It is through the *adbhuta rasa* that the love of Parvati ultimately leads to Shiva's self realisation transforming her into the supreme Shaivite goddess of love. Shaivism with its distinctive world-view and metaphysics, its unique sectarian rites and rituals, its religious icons and artistic images, while retaining the overall ethos of Hinduism, stands on its own, and in its manifold world, Parvati the goddess of love truly presides. When it comes to the mundane and everyday world of the Indian woman, Parvati does not remain a distant goddess but emerges as an intimate and empathetic friend in whom she can confide. The common Indian woman, far from the sophistication of art and liturgy considers Parvati a true and loving friend, in whom she can confide and whose example she wishes to emulate in her life, especially in her marriage, through the celebration of *vratas*, vows, and festivals.

The Sanskritic Tradition

The story of Parvati's life, as for all Hindus, begins even before she is born.

Shiva's first consort Sati had immolated herself at her father Daksha's *yajna*, fire sacrifice. The inconsolable Shiva carried her charred body in his *bhairava tandava*, dance of rage, and then retreated despairingly into his inward, ascetic meditation in Kailasa. The gods remained concerned at Shiva's uninvolvement with the world and his indifference to the ravages that the demon Taraka was unleashing on the three worlds. Seeking succour they approached Aditi, the primal mother goddess and asked her to enter the womb of Mena, the queen of Himachal, the mountain king. Thus even as Parvati was conceived she knew that she was destined to be Shiva's wife. The mother goddess reminded Mena that it was she herself that was in Mena's womb. Parvati was born at midnight when the constellation Mrigashiras was in conjunction with the moon on the ninth day in the month of Madhu, in the season of spring. The gods sounded drums, the celestial Gandharvas sang songs and flowers fell from the sky. Lotuses bloomed, gentle breezes blew and people rejoiced. Himachal named his daughter Kali and the young child grew in beauty day by day, just as the moon increases in splendour night after night. The child was fondly attached to everyone, not only of the family but of the entire town, and it was thus that she was called Parvati, a name befitting the family that resided in the mountain. The infant Parvati was beautiful and charming and was raised with much love and affection by her father Himachal and mother Mena. She grew up to be sensually beautiful and spiritually adept. She mastered the various aspects of yoga and spent time in the worship of Shiva in his aniconic *linga* form. Just as the flock of swans returns to the Ganga in the autumn so also all the learning of her previous birth returned to Parvati. At an appropriate time Himachal approached the sage Narada and asked that he read the horoscope of his daughter. Narada on reading the horoscope said she had a very auspicious future and that all except her marriage line were favourable, for her husband would be a naked ascetic without a father or a mother. While Himachal and Mena were distressed to hear this prediction, Narada assuaged them by saying that such an ascetic was none other than the great god Shiva, and that their love would be immortal. Himachal asked Narada how an ascetic who had abandoned the world and who was given to inward contemplation and meditation could make a good husband for his lovely and charming daughter. Narada revealed to Himachal the fact that Parvati was none other than Sati reborn. Pacified, Himachal put Parvati lovingly on his knee. The departing Narada assured the parents that Parvati would have a better throne than this, for Shiva's thigh would be her permanent abode, and that she would go to the world where no eye or mind can reach.

Mena's doubts about Shiva as a future husband for her daughter persisted and she asked her husband to get Parvati married to a handsome bridegroom instead. Himachal assured her that none other than Shiva would be their son-in-law and that to obtain Shiva Parvati would have to perform severe penance. He also spoke of a dream he had in which Shiva arrived near their city to perform penance and had a discourse with their daughter, where he expounded the magnificence of *Vedanta* and Parvati that of *Sankhya*. He assured Mena that once Parvati commenced her penance the beneficial results would follow.

Himachal's dream came true and Shiva, accompanied by his trusted Nandi and two attendants, *ganas*, came to Aushadiprastha to practice austerities. Parvati, with her two *sakhis*, friends, Jaya and Vijaya gently approached Shiva with fruits and flowers, and while Shiva did catch a glimpse of her beauty he could not be disturbed from his deep meditation. Shiva admonished Himachal that his daughter, a slender bodied maiden of comely hips and moon-like face, should not be brought to his presence, for a woman is an illusion, who fosters worldliness and from whose contact virtuous penance is destroyed. On hearing this Parvati addressed Shiva and explained that the energy behind every activity was *prakriti*, and that it is *prakriti* that creates, sustains and destroys everything that is embodied. Parvati explained that while Shiva was the pristine *purusha* she was the primordial *prakriti*. Hearing this powerful exposition of the *Sankhya* doctrine from Parvati, a doctrine which upholds the role of matter as *prakriti*, Shiva upheld the Vedantin's point of view which gives primacy to the pure, subjective and majestic *purusha* unsullied by *prakriti*, and continued his solitary inward meditation. Parvati was unperturbed and continued to serve Shiva. She washed Shiva's feet and drank that holy water. Worshipping him with sixteen types of offerings everyday she would return home only to return the next day.

While Himachal and Mena were discouraged at the outcome of Parvati's service, Parvati merely engaged in more penance to win the heart of Shiva, for her mission in life was to marry him, and to this end no austerity was too great or too severe for her. Parvati, who was also a *tapasvani*, knew only too well that no *sadhana* or spiritual effort would be complete without *tapasya*, that no effort would bear fruit unless undertaken in a spirit of selflessness, sacrifice and dedication. She would immerse herself in a pool of cold water standing on one leg for days on end. She would live only on leaves that had fallen on the ground, a practice that earned her the name of Aparna. But Shiva remained unmoved.

The gods approached Kama the God of Love to shoot arrows of love into Shiva. Kama took up his bow made up of *kinshuka* flowers with bees for its bowstring and shot five arrows made of *aravindam, ashoka, chutam, navamallika* and *nilotphala* flowers. Kama's arrows angered Shiva who opened his third eye and burnt Kama to ashes. Kama's death saddened Parvati who could find no happiness or peace in her heart. She left home and went to a holy place on the mountain to perform further penance. She stood for a while at Gaurishikhara in the place where Shiva had performed penance and became dispirited by pangs of separation from him. She built an altar there and commenced her penance. In the summer she surrounded herself by blazing fires; in the monsoon she let herself be drenched; in the chilly winter she immersed herself in water and when the snow fell she fasted. Performing such austerities and constantly chanting the five syllabled mantra *aum namo shivaya* she meditated on Shiva with single-minded concentration. Meanwhile the flower arrows produced the desired result and Shiva was aroused and attracted romantically and lustfully towards Parvati. When he saw Parvati, Shiva spoke of her beauty: Her face is like the moon, her eyes like lotus petals, her eyebrows are the bows of Kama, her lower lip like the *bimba* fruit, her nose like the beak of a parrot, her voice like the cooing of a cuckoo, her slender waist like the sacrificial altar. No other person equalled her beauty in the three worlds. However even though Shiva was aroused from his slumberous meditation and attracted to Parvati he was beset by doubts and undertook to test Parvati's resolve. Disguising himself as an ascetic he approached Parvati and asked why she was undertaking such severe penance for a man as unworthy as Shiva. Parvati was unmoved and reaffirmed her resolve to marry Shiva and no-one else. Shiva, pleased, revealed himself to Parvati.

On the day of the wedding Aushadiprastha was bedecked with flowers and festoons and the entire town teemed with excitement hitherto unseen. Every vantage point on the route of the marriage procession was taken and women stood in balconies to catch a glimpse of the bride and the groom. Shiva came with a large retinue of *ganas* and other attendants, and his constant companion Nandi, the bull. As the ritual fires were lit Brahma officiated. Vishnu gave the shy and demure Parvati away. Following custom Parvati led Shiva in the final round around the holy fire, thus becoming *vama,* the one who occupies the position on Shiva's left.

Shiva was passionate in his love for Parvati and the honeymoon was joyous and sensual. There were amorous games and lover's quarrels but the marriage was a happy one with both Shiva and Parvati dallying romantically in the idyllic Kailasa mountains. Of the many games they played the one of great significance was *chaupat,* the dice game. Narada went to see Shiva in Kailasa and found that he was in his chambers with Parvati. He approached them and said that rather than making love they should play *chaupat.* Parvati was angered by Narada's suggestion but then agreed to play. Initially she lost to Shiva but then gradually the tables turned and Shiva lost everything he had staked in the game including the crescent moon, his necklace and earrings. When Parvati demanded that Shiva give her everything he had staked there was a fight between the two, much to the anguish of Narada and Shiva's trusted devotee Bhringi. Parvati removed Shiva's snake, the crescent moon and even his loincloth. Bhringi was put to shame and Shiva too was enraged and opened his third eye. The two separated. Shiva retreated into the wilderness and Parvati went into her quarters. She was tormented by this separation and at the bidding of her companions Jaya and Vijaya went in search of Shiva. She took the form of a *shabari,* a tribal woman, and approached Shiva who was deep in meditation. Shiva was attracted towards the *shabari* but when he realised that she was none other than Parvati realised his mistake and united with her much to their joy.

There were also many moments of philosophical discourse between the two. While Shiva taught Parvati the doctrine of *Vedanta,* Parvati responded by teaching him the doctrines of *Sankhya,* for if Shiva as Dakshinamurti was the perfect teacher, Parvati as a *yogini* was no less. Parvati was constantly by Shiva's side helping, encouraging, assisting, participating in every activity of his.

Parvati's sojourn in Kailasa was to witness a big battle with the demon king Jalandhara. Jalandhara was the son of the ocean, brother of Lakshmi. He had defeated Vishnu in battle and ruled over the three worlds. The gods were distressed at their plight and approached Shiva who in turn asked the sage Narada to intervene on their behalf and destroy Jalandhara. Narada hatched a plot to engage Jalandhara in battle with Shiva, a battle that would eventually lead to the destruction of this demon king. Approaching Jalandhara in his kingdom Narada said that while he had every material possession in the world, Shiva's abode in Kailasa was better than his. Kailasa, said Narada, was ten thousand *yojanas* wide, has a grove of *kalpa* trees, hundreds of *kamadhenus*, wish-fulfilling cows, and was illuminated by Chintamani gems brilliant with gold. Hearing this Jalandhara decided to show his prosperity to Narada. He said that there was none greater than him for he had usurped the elephant of Indra, the swan-chariot of Brahma, the Parijat tree, the Mahapadma of Kubera, the umbrella of Varuna and the javelin of Mratyu. Narada was impressed by all this but told Jalandhara that he lacked the greatest treasure of Shiva and that was Parvati. On hearing this Jalandhara was enraged and deputed his assistant Rahu to go to Kailasa and bring Parvati to his court. Rahu approached Shiva and said that his master Jalandhara was the king of the three worlds and the only thing missing in his court was Parvati. "What use to you, a wandering ash-covered ascetic, is the exquisitely beautiful Parvati?" Hearing this Shiva was angered and Rahu trembled and took refuge at Shiva's feet and returned to Jalandhara. When Jalandhara heard this account of Rahu's defeat he was furious and commanded that his entire army be marshalled to defeat Shiva and bring Parvati to his court. The army of *asuras*, demons, led by Jalandhara and with Kalanemi, Shumba, Nishumba, Daurhrdas, Kalakas, Mauryas and Dhaumars and a host of others, laid siege to Kailasa. Shiva commanded his army of *ganas*, Ganesha and Kartikeya and Nandi and a terrible battle was fought. Weapons clashed with weapons, the whole earth shook with the sounds of war drums and conches and the space between heaven and earth became enveloped by arrows. When the armies were exhausted it was time for a direct battle between Jalandhara and Shiva. Finding that he was no match for the prowess of Shiva, Jalandhara tried in one last vain attempt to defeat Shiva. By the power of his *maya,* illusions, he created hosts of *gandharvas* and celestial damsels to distract Shiva. While Shiva was engrossed with the *gandharvas* playing flutes and cymbals, Jalandhara disguised himself as Shiva and went towards Parvati. However Parvati was not fooled and eventually Jalandhara was slain by Shiva.

Having eliminated the powerful Jalandhara, Shiva and Parvati resumed their sojourn in Kailasa, sporting, dallying and discoursing. Parvati was constantly by Shiva's side, taking part in every activity. An important part of Shiva'a daily routine was the preparation of *bhang,* his favourite intoxicant. Parvati would lovingly collect the best *bhang* leaves, crush them and then filter the decoction through a clean muslin cloth. At other times Parvati would help Shiva make a quilt that would keep them warm in the cold nights in Kailasa. At yet other times she would sit by his feet massaging them while Shiva reclined under a tree. Parvati's greatest pleasure was to serve Shiva and cater to his every need. Nothing was more important to her than being useful to her lord, tending to his every comfort and ensuring that he would not lapse into his solitary, self-denying ascetic ways. In these activities she combined the roles of a caring wife and an affectionate mother.

While Parvati exulted in her romantic dalliance with Shiva the true mother in her longed for a child. She would entreat Shiva to beget a son and make her a mother but the ascetic Shiva would hear nothing of it. She reminded Shiva that no ancestral rituals are performed for a man who has no descendants. Shiva assured her that he had no desire to be a *grahastha,* householder, for such a state in life brings fetters. Parvati was disheartened and seeing her in that state Shiva pulled a thread out of her red dress and made a son and gave it to her. Parvati held him to her breast and he came to life. As he sucked on her milk he smiled and Parvati, pleased, gave the son to Shiva. Shiva was surprised that Parvati had breathed life in a child made of fabric but warned that the planet Saturn would prove inauspicious for this child and as he spoke those words the child's head fell to the ground. Parvati was overcome with grief. Shiva tried unsuccessfully to put the head back together. A voice in the sky said that only the head of someone facing north would stick to this child. Shiva deputed Nandi to find such a person. Nandi soon found Indra's elephant Airavat lying with his head facing north and began to cut it. Indra intervened but Nandi was eventually successful, although in the struggle one of the tusks of the elephant was broken. Nandi took the head to Shiva and thus was born Ganesha. The gods celebrated the birth and Parvati was pleased.

Once Parvati found Shiva in an amorous mood and the two were together in erotic love-play. So long were they together that the gods were troubled, for the demon Taraka was still unconquered and the gods went with Brahma to take refuge in Vishnu. Vishnu went with his entourage of gods to Kailasa and waited patiently outside the quarters of Shiva. Many years passed and yet Shiva was closeted with Parvati. Vishnu spoke in a shrill and plaintive voice and entreated Shiva to come out and listen to their problem. When Shiva disregarded this Agni disguised himself as a pigeon and entered the bed chamber of Shiva. Parvati immediately sensed that her privacy was violated. Shiva withdrew and a drop of his semen fell on the ground. Agni in the form of the dove ate the drop of semen. Parvati however was disturbed and angry that the gods had assembled and interrupted her erotic pleasures, and cursed them that all their wives would be barren. She was particularly enraged at Agni for having eaten the seed of Shiva.

When Agni was unable to bear the fiery seed he went to the banks of the Ganga. It was summer and the wives of the seven sages had come to the Ganga at dawn to bathe. Six of the wives felt cold and went towards Agni. Agni dropped the seed and the seed entered the wives through their hair and they became pregnant. When the sages found this out they admonished their wives who placed the embryo on one of the peaks of the Himalayas. Thus was born Kartikeya, a lustrous child with six heads. Shiva and Parvati were delighted at the birth of their son and it added much joy to Parvati who had longed for a child.

Parvati had a third child, Andhaka, and the story of his birth took place on Mount Mandara where the divine couple were sporting. In jest Parvati closed Shiva's eyes with her delicate hands and at once a vast darkness engulfed the world. The hands of the goddess were drenched in Shiva's fluid born of passion and when this was heated by the heat of Shiva's third eye it grew into a horrific child, blind and gruesome. Parvati lovingly cared for this child as well, but as Andhaka grew he became a demon lusting for his own mother and was eventually put to death by Shiva.

Parvati had an ambiguous relationship to her Lord's devotees who were both mythic and historical. One such devotee was Bhringi who had a single-minded devotion to Shiva and did not recognise Parvati at all. He would worship only Shiva and when Parvati became *ardhanari* Bhringi became a bee to avoid circumambulating Parvati, going between Shiva and Parvati's heads. Parvati cursed him and Bhringi became mere bones and lost all his flesh. Shiva gave him a third leg. However Sambandar another ardent devotee of Shiva of the 7th century, and a child-saint roused Parvati's maternal instinct. He was given milk as he sat on the steps of a Shiva temple crying with hunger.

Shiva's ascetic nature could never be completely hidden and even after his marriage he would be given to periods of quietitude and isolation when he would leave Parvati and retreat into his meditation. While Parvati understood this need and would even encourage him, her mother Mena would be distraught at the fate of her daughter.

Thus Parvati happily spent her life in Kailasa giving totally of herself and of her love, now in the service of her Lord, now in the company of her children, ever-mindful of her duties and responsibilities, remaining ever-resplendent as the primordial *prakriti*.

The Tamil Tradition

The narrative of Parvati takes on a different colour in Tamil country. This region was dominated by Jains till the 4th century and it was not until the 5th century that there was a Hindu renaissance. While Shaivism had existed for many centuries prior to this, it was only under the influence of *brahmins* from the north, that the importance of Parvati grew. The sources of Tamil culture are to be found in the secular Sangam literature of the beginning of the millennium, the two epics *Silappadikaram* and *Manimekalai*, the hymns of the Tevaram and in the *sthalapurana* or local legends of each shrine. While the literature had multiple layers of nuance and meaning it was the *sthalapuranas* that took shape after the 9th century that gave each shrine a special sanctity. This was due mainly to the Shaivite saints or the Nayanmars, who sang separately about each shrine.

As with the northern *Puranas* the central theme in the Tamil myths is also the marriage of Shiva and Parvati. Their wedding in

Tamil accounts is considered to be their second, the first having taken place in Kailasa. The story is told of Agastya, the dwarf-sage who was exiled to the south to maintain a balance as the entire world had gathered in Kailasa to celebrate the wedding of Shiva and Parvati. The weight of so many people in the north unbalanced the subcontinent and Agastya was deputed by Shiva to go south to maintain the balance. Agastya did as he was commanded and worshipping at all the Shiva shrines along the way reached a forest where he felt peace. He dug up a *linga* at the base of a great tree. Shiva blessed him and soon he got a vision of Parvati in her wedding sari. Agastya combined the learning of both Tamil and Sanskrit and his arrival in the south from the north is seen not only as the starting point of Tamil culture but an admission that the Tamil myths were derived from a northern source. Brahminism was the inspiring and fertilising source of Tamil culture, but Tamil myths under its patronage were able to develop their unique flavour. Tamil myths are more closely tied to temple worship than the Sanskrit *Puranas* and are meant to encourage the devotee to undertake a pilgrimage to that shrine and experience first-hand the power implicit in the shrine.

Tamil culture asserts the immanence rather than the transcendence of Shiva, his particular rather than his universal presence in a specific shrine, and this further explains the importance that is attached to an individual shrine and to the devotion it creates and expects from its devotees. In a typical Tamilian explanation it is said that even though the whole cow is filled with milk, milk is available only through the udders; thus it is that Shiva and Parvati though universal are available only in a particular shrine, and that too only through Parvati. Another common feature of the Tamil myths is that they are centred not around Shiva but around Parvati and her various manifestations.

It is she who provides *pratistha*, the firm ground of stability, that makes life for Shiva and his devotees possible in the shrine despite the chaos around it. Parvati further demarcates the shrine to protect it from the surroundings and ensures that the shrine is the centre of the universe.

The three main shrines that are associated with Parvati in Tamil Nadu are those at Madurai, Kanchi and Chidambaram where she not only takes on a different name but a special persona in her relation to Shiva. Thus Parvati goes by the name Minakshi, Kamakshi, Nilayatakshi and so on.

Most myths, and Tamil myths are no exception, begin with a story of a flood. It is said that Parvati descended to earth from Kailasa to expiate the sin of closing the eyes of Shiva. She worshipped Shiva in the form of a *linga*, at Kanchi, and he in order to test her, gathered all the waters of the world and poured them into the river Kampai which flooded the town of Kanchi. Parvati embraced the *linga* to save it from the deluge and it is said that it is because of this that the *linga* at Kanchi bears the marks of her breasts and bracelets. In sharing the universal flood myths, the temples of Tamil Nadu are tied to the entire cosmogony of creation and destruction, and the shrine itself is considered to be the centre of the universe.

While the marriage of Parvati is central to the Tamil myths, as it is in the Sanskrit *Puranas*, there are significant differences between the two traditions. In the Sanskritic tradition it is Shiva who has a double persona, the erotic and the ascetic, while Parvati is the romantic consort. In the Tamil myths it is Parvati who has two sides to her personality, one a dark, violent, erotic and potentially dangerous side, the other a bright, quiet, romantic and benevolent side. The first is the southern goddess who arises from the dark womb of the earth, the second, the northern one who lives in the idyllic Kailasa. It is generally accepted that Shiva who is initially married in Kailasa to the romantic Parvati is married a second time to the southern more aggressive goddess in Tamil Nadu. The southern goddess is a complex amalgam of destruction and creation, violence and benevolence, chaos and order, and in this respect resembles more the goddess of the folk tradition than the classical Sanskritic northern goddess who is purely romantic. While northern Shaivism is romantic and soft the Tamil Shaiva tradition, in incorporating this dark goddess, is more life-affirming and not separable from the dark and violent aspects of life. Another difference is that while in the Sanskritic *Puranas* the gods encourage Parvati to marry Shiva so that the demon Taraka can be killed by Shiva's son, in the Tamil myths gods and men alike seek to keep the goddess a virgin so that she can preserve her strength to fight enemies. Preserving Parvati's virginity in Tamil myths is important to safeguard and protect both gods and humans, for virginity ensures that the goddess will not squander her strength and power. While unmarried goddesses are considered dangerous and even malicious in the Tamil tradition, married goddesses are expected to preserve their virginity.

A Tamil myth describes how Shiva wanted to marry the goddess at Kanyakumari. The gods were alarmed at the prospect of the goddess losing her virginity and therefore deputed Narada to intervene. Narada insisted that Shiva bring with him for the marriage coconuts without eyes, mangoes without seeds and betel leaves without veins. Shiva was able to gather these unusual things and set out to marry Kanyakumari at the appointed hour of midnight. Narada then took the form of a rooster and announced the hour of dawn. Shiva believed that the auspicious hour had passed and turned back. Kanyakumari waited until dawn, was disappointed that Shiva did not come, and it is said that she waits even today.

Parvati as Minakshi makes a late appearance in Tamil country as the early Shaiva literature is male dominant. In early Sangam literature the only reference to Shiva's consort is to a goddess, Kotravai, who was later allied to Kali rather than to Parvati, who keeps the rhythm when Shiva dances or who as *ardhanari* resides in one half of Shiva. Ilango in his 2nd century AD epic *Silappadikaram* refers to the goddess of Madurai who is to become the consort of Shiva. The 7th century poet saint Jnanasambandar continues this reference of the consort of Shiva in his songs of praise to his beloved Shiva. It is only after the sixteenth century that Tamil poets began to glorify the beauty and grace of Parvati. Two such well-known works are *Minakshi Ammai Pillai* by Kumara Guruparar and *Abhirami Andhati* by Abhirami Pattar.

It is only in the seventeenth century Tamil *sthalapurana Tiruvilaiyatrapuranam* or *Shiva's Sacred Games* by Paranjyoti Munivar that the entire narrative of Minakshi unfolds, and this text becomes the central *purana* of the Minakshi temple of Madurai. It was about this time in the history of the Tamil country that Tirumalai Nayak ascended the throne of Madurai and it was he who conceived of the grand festival. Madurai was traditionally regarded as the seat of Tamil culture and it is but fitting that the narrative from this important text unfolds in Madurai. Paranjyoti's work it is said was divinely inspired but drew upon earlier Tamil and Sanskrit Shaiva literature and as the *sthalapurana* of the Minakshi temple in Madurai it is venerated by devotees. The King of Madurai, Malayadhvaja Pandya, was childless and offered a number of horse sacrifices to beget a son. After the ninety-ninth such sacrifice, Indra fearing that if the king completed a hundred sacrifices he would be able to claim his own throne, suggested to Malayadhvaja that he perform another type of sacrifice that would beget him a son. Malayadhvaja did as we was told and the result was that a three-year-old daughter with three breasts was born. The king was depressed and lamented at the birth of such a freak child. At that point he heard Shiva's voice which exhorted the king to raise the child as a son and further predicted that when she would meet her Lord the third breast would disappear. The king did as he was told and raised his daughter as if she were the male heir to the throne. The child had large round eyes like those of a fish and was given the name Minakshi or the fish-eyed one. Soon after the coronation of Minakshi as the queen of Madurai the king died.

The central theme of *Shiva's Sacred Games* is the marriage of Shiva and Parvati and in the fifth chapter of this book the narrative opens with Minakshi, the Pandya queen of Madurai, ruling her kingdom. She is unmarried, and while this causes anxiety to her mother Kanchanamalai, Minakshi is determined to conquer the world. She assembles her army and sets out to subdue the eight guardian deities. Indra flees at the sight of her troops and his white elephant Airavat and *kalpavriksha* are taken by Minakshi as booty. Minakshi's troops march to Kailasa the abode of Shiva. A great battle ensues between Minakshi and Nandi and Nandi's forces are completely routed. Shiva enters the fray at this stage and when Minakshi sees him her third breast disappears. At this point she becomes bashful, leans unsteadily, her long hair falls on her neck and she scratches the earth with her toes. This was the moment that Minakshi's minister Sumati had predicted. She falls in love with Shiva and Shiva agrees to come to Madurai to marry her. Minakshi returns to Madurai and the town is in a frenzy at hearing the news. There are celebrations everywhere and preparations are made for the ensuing marriage. Shiva advances to Madurai with his wedding party which includes Vishnu and Brahma and the women of Madurai are filled with lust at the sight of the handsome bridegroom. Shiva is honoured by the *brahmins* of Madurai, while Vishnu washes Shiva's feet and the assembled deities drink this sacred water. Brahma is the officiating priest and Vishnu gives away the bride. Shiva ties the wedding necklace on Minakshi and points to the pole star and leads his bride into the marriage chamber. As Shiva prepares to take his place on the throne as the king of the Pandya empire he bestows gifts to the assembled guests and instructs them on just kingship.

It is important to understand the role Vishnu plays at Minakshi's wedding. In Tamil mythology Vishnu is regarded as Minakshi's brother and it is she who brings peace to the ambiguous relationship between Shiva and Vishnu. There are many instances of conflict between Shiva and Vishnu, both in the north and the south, and many stories that bring about a reconciliation between the two. However in the marriage of Minakshi there is not only a rapprochement between the two but there is now a relationship; Shiva becomes Vishnu's brother-in-law.

The wedding transformed the assembled guests to divinity and Madurai became the centre of the universe. The text says that Shiva as Somasundara took his seat on the throne as a Pandya king, his flag with the roaring bull became the flag with the beautiful fish, snake ornaments became ornaments of gold, blossoming laburnum flowers became margosa blossoms, tiger skin clothing became golden attire, the crescent moon in his hair became a diamond-studded crown, and then, according to the scriptures, he built, in Madurai, a Shiva temple. The wedding and its annual celebration is a central event in the lives of the citizens of Madurai.

Kinship terms are an important part of the Hindu social and family tradition. Suffixed to a name the kinship term adds a certain emotional content to that relationship. The Tamil Shaiva tradition extends this practice even to deities who then become more approachable. Minakshi is the beloved daughter of the people of Madurai and Shiva the honoured *marukan*, son-in-law. It is this kinship that underpins the entire ritual, liturgy, theology and devotion to Minakshi in Madurai and helps in the understanding and celebration of the marriage. Minakshi, to the people of Madurai and to all her devotees, is a daughter first and deity next. She is the one who is worshipped first and it is she who is the devotee's emissary to Shiva. There is a sense of family about Minakshi, Shiva and the people of Madurai. By entering into a marriage alliance with the daughter of the Pandya king Shiva ensures the welfare of the kingdom. Marriage for Shiva, as it is for humans, becomes quintessentially a religious act. Marriage as a sacrament of life is equivalent to a *yajna,* sacrifice, and it is a time when the difference between the human and the divine is blurred. It is interesting to note that while in the northern Sanskritic tradition Shiva has an adversarial relationship with his in-laws, in the south this relationship is affectionate and fond.

While Minakshi embodies the regal grace of a queen as well as that of the consort of Shiva, Kamakshi epitomises the erotic aspect of the goddess. Kamakshi, so called because she has the eyes of desire, is the passionate goddess. One of the Tamil myths recounts how after Kama was burned by Shiva, his ashes entered into the limbs of Kamakshi and the goddess thus revived him. Her association with Kama is carried into her iconography as she, like Kama, is shown carrying a bow of sugarcane and arrows of flowers. In bringing Kama back to life again Kamakshi secures her own advantage, for Kama is once again able to discharge his flower arrow which compels Shiva to go to the goddess seeking her love. Kamakshi is thus able to tame the mighty Shiva not through her *tapas* but through her erotic power.

Whether it is the regal Minakshi or the erotic Kamakshi, there are certain features of Tamil myths which set the southern goddess apart from the softer northern Parvati. The southern goddess is a source of violent and erotic power which ultimately tames the mighty Shiva into submission. She is a dark bride who combines both creation and destruction, her strength is her virginity which must be protected at all times, her womb is the dark earth in which she locates Shiva.

The Folk Tradition

The folk tradition of India is made up by a disparate group of people. It includes not only nomads and tribals, gypsies and wanderers, best described by the generic term *adivasis* or first settlers, but equally women in settled areas who rely more on the oral rather than the Shastraic canonical tradition. While the folk tradition permeates all levels of life and living it is particularly rich when it comes to the celebration of the goddess. The godhead of Shiva is prehistoric and the image of a cross-legged *yogi* seen in the seals of the Indus Valley civilisation are considered those of a proto-Shiva. It has also been suggested that images of a human with a bow and arrow in the rock paintings of Bhimbetka in Central India, dating back to the same period or even beyond, are those of a Shiva-like figure. Although there seems to have been at that time a cult of mother goddesses and tree nymphs, there is no definite evidence of a consort of Shiva. However, as the folk tradition developed and grew, it incorporated not only local legends and popular stories into its fold, but also appropriated to itself some of the features of the classical Sanskritic and Tamil traditions, yet maintaining its unique autochthonous ethos.

A feature of the folk goddess is that she is very often an amalgam of all the four consorts of Shiva, and in particular an admixture of Parvati and Durga. While the classical Sanskritic tradition keeps Parvati and Durga separate the folk tradition generally accepts a composite goddess that displays the persona of both. The folk goddess is therefore an overarching goddess who is both romantic and valiant, protector and destroyer, motherly and martial at the same time. Unlike the classical tradition the folk tradition is kept alive by household observances, social events and village festivals.

One such folk equivalent of Shiva and Parvati in Maharashtra and Karnataka is Khandoba, also called Mallari, Mallayya, Mahabaleshwar and his consort Mahalsa, also called Malardevi, Malchi, Malvi and Mahalaya. Khandoba is one of many tribal deities that comes closest to the Puranic Shiva. Khandoba for the tribals is the killer of demons. The *Brahmandapurana* contains a subtext called Mallari Mahatmya that mentions that Khandoba killed the demons Mani and Malla when the *rishis* called on him for help. While Khandoba is the killer of demons he is also associated with mountains, for a mountain is the tribal phallic equivalent of a *linga*. Khandoba's status as a deity, even within the folk tradition, shifts from his originally being a god of the tribals to his becoming a god of settled communities like the Dhangars. This transformation of Khandoba, it has been suggested, is the function of his consorts. Unlike the Sanskritic tradition Khandoba has two consorts, one from the higher and the other from the lower social strata. The first consort comes from a higher caste. She is Sanskritised and is therefore more in accord with the Brahmanical pantheon, the second consort is from a lower caste. The origin of the first consort Mhalsa is tied interestingly to Mohini and thus to Vishnu. Folk legend has it that when Vishnu took the form of Mohini during the *samudra manthan*, churning of the ocean, to distract the *asuras*, Shiva was also attracted to her. Unable to give herself to Shiva, Mohini promised Shiva that in her next incarnation she would return as his consort. Mhalsa is that reincarnation of Mohini born in the village of Nevas to a merchant called Timmaseth. Mhalsa, besides being worshiped as the consort of Khandoba, also acquired the status of an independent *gramadevi*, a village goddess, and is worshipped even today in Paithan, Nandev, Nevas and Mhardol. While Mhalsa is from the higher Lingayat caste, Khandoba also takes on a second consort from the Dhangar pastoral caste. This pastoral consort takes on the legends and folklore of the region and is called variously Balai, Banai or Bajubai. The two consorts, Mhalsa and Banai are thus the folk equivalents of Parvati.

Banai was married to Khandoba by *gandharva* rites by the herdsmen. It is said that at the wedding of Khandoba and Banai no wedding band played and the only music was that of the bleating of sheep. Sheep dung was tossed at the ceremony instead of rice. After the ceremony Khandoba and Banai went to Jejuri which even today is the centre of the Khandoba cult in Maharashtra. Khandoba's vehicle is not the bull but the horse, once again in keeping with his function as a god of the pastoral communities. Khandoba is venerated through songs and ritually celebrated even today through worship at various temples dedicated to him. The villagers show their allegiance to him by placing memorial stones in the vicinity of the temple bearing, besides the name of the deceased, a sculpting of the Uma-Maheshvara motif on the stone. Even in death the folk tradition preserves its own unique identity, for memorial stones are not commonly seen in the Sanskritic tradition.

If Mhalsa is the Deccani equivalent of Parvati, in the hills of Kumaon she is Nandadevi, the mountain goddess. Worshipped and venerated in shrines that dot the hills and valleys of Kumaon, the central event that celebrates Nandadevi is a pilgrimage in which the goddess undertakes a journey in a palanquin as a divine bride and is taken back to her husband's home. Nandadevi's annual pilgrimage which takes place in the month of *bhado* (August–September), called *Shri Nandadevi raj jat yatra* is observed with religious passion and fervour and touches the lives of the mountain people in a number of different ways the most important being the outpouring of filial love of the women of the Kumaon hills for Nandavevi. It is important to note that this festival is significantly different from *navratra* which is observed in the month of *ashvin* (October) and which centres round the worship of Durga. For these women of Kumaon Nandadevi is a goddess, a daughter of the village and a beloved sister, whose departure from their midst to her husbands's home in Kailasa is cause for pain and anguish. There is in this event none of the objectivity, sophistication and detachment of the classical tradition, for this pilgrimage becomes, for the women of Kumaon a stylised version of their own post-marital journey from their natal home to that of their husbands. In this scenario Nandadevi becomes a reluctant goddess that goes back to Shiva. The pilgrims that carry the palanquin and others who join take on the persona of Nandadevi's natal relatives and express their sadness at her going away.

In folklore as opposed to *purana*, myth politics and kinship get intermingled. It has rightly been said that a world-view is not valid until it is publicly expressed. The repressed emotions of the women of Kumaon who live in a male dominated world and away from their natal relatives are vividly expressed in song and dance at this annual pilgrimage. This pilgrimage of Nandadevi has a metasocial and reflexive significance and like other pilgrimages in India, has an intrinsic religious power and strength for the people that participate in it. Furthermore the ambience of the mountains in which it takes place gives it greater sanctity for, after all, Parvati is a daughter of the mountains. Processions have a special way of uniting the people who participate in them. What it lacks in refinement the procession more than makes up in drama, and it keeps alive Nandadevi in the minds and hearts of people. In expressing their love for Nandadevi the women of Kumaon are empowered, for Nandadevi, in receiving the love and adulation, the anguish and the pathos, reflects it back and makes a social statement on their behalf, letting them maintain their ties to their natal place. So when the women of the Kuamon chant "Bhagawati ki jai ho" they are wishing for their own victory as much as that of the goddess.

In Maharashtra Parvati is celebrated as Gauri. Images of Gauri are made either from a handful of earth, by decorating a shrub with a mask and fabric, or by assembling five stones from the river. Gauri is ritually worshipped during the annual Ganesha festival in the month of *bhadrapad* (August), and in the Haritalilka homecoming festival in *chaitra* (April) when it is believed that Gauri returns to her natal home for a month. Gauri is a fertility goddess ensuring prosperity to the farmer, a happy marriage to the bride and equally a friend to the ordinary women who toil in the fields and work in the home.

In Rajasthan Parvati is celebrated as Gangaur and at this festival folk images of Parvati are made, bedecked with clothes and jewellery and processed through the streets. It is a festival not only for commoners but equally for the nobility.

In all her folk manifestations the image of Parvati is that of a dedicated and loving wife whose presence for the women is that of a trusted friend, whose example is worthy of being emulated by every bride and whose very being is an offering to Shiva's happiness and eventual self-realisation. What the classical tradition achieves through erudite scriptures and sophisticated imagery the folk tradition imbibes with robust enthusiasm, earthy spontaneity and simple rituals.

The Literature of Parvati

Under the generic term *devisahitya* there is a vast corpus of literature of the goddess that straddles both the sacred and the secular, ancient and modern. The overlap between different goddesses and especially between the *shaktis,* consorts of Shiva, is perhaps more evident in literature than in plastic or pictorial images. The cohesion is particularly marked between Parvati and Durga as the dividing line between them gets hazy. Even more interestingly Parvati, who belongs to the Shaivite tradition, is sometimes given a Vaishnavite colouring in some songs. Despite these ambiguities Parvati in and of herself, and in her own right, has a secure place in literature. In prose and poetry, through songs and drama, she is eulogised and celebrated in many different ways. In gathering and sifting through this literature one is constantly aware that the extant literature is only a small part of what must have been written, and even more so, many songs and stories of Parvati form a part of the rich, diverse and vast oral tradition. In some ways this applies more to Parvati than any other goddess. She has inspired not only poets and princes but common peasants and the proletariat, not only the women of the nobility but equally the common household woman. She is remembered not only at fairs and festivals but equally at bazaars and weddings, not just at courts but equally in homes and *havelis*. For Parvati is the darling of the community, dear to poets, a friend of the common woman, an inspiration for *rasikas*. And for Parvati, as it is in the Indian arts in general, this rich oral tradition remains the bedrock of the various visual and performing arts.

Head of Gauri
Contemporary
Collection: Harsha Dehejia

The *Puranas*, and the *Shiv Purana* in particular, must be regarded as the earliest literature of Parvati, for it is here that her life is chronicled, her persona revealed and her marriage to Shiva eulogised. Parvati is referred to in other *Puranas* as well, especially *Agni Purana*, *Padma Purana*, and *Skanda Purana*. The tone of the *Shiv Purana* is poetic, the style narrative and the attitude is one of loving tribute to a goddess who is also a daughter, of a consort who is also a *nayika*, of a demure wife who is frightened and runs to Shiva's side when accosted by a demon rather than rushing to kill the demon, who holds a mirror or a flower rather than a *trishul* or battle axe, who prefers to remain in the romantic surroundings of Kailasa rather than seek the battle-field or the cremation ground. This is totally different from the later *Devi Mahatmya* which catalogues Durga's valiant and martial deeds and worships and venerates her. And in many ways this romantic and soft ambience of the *Shiv Purana* sets the tone for the literature that follows.

Classical Sanskrit literature grew in the ambience of courts and is in the form of poetry or drama and not prose. Classical poets were never far from mythology or philosophy and therefore the distinction between the sacred and the secular in this genre of literature is redundant, for the two were part of an integral whole. They moved easily from one to the other, for now Parvati is a romantic *nayika* and now she is a goddess in the hands of these poets. While placing their creation in the general frame of the *Shiva Purana* each poet excelled in their own way in one of many aspects of Parvati's persona.

A survey of the literature on Parvati must begin with Kalidasa. The opening lines of *Raghuvamsha* "*vagarthaiva sampraktau... vande parvati paremshvarau*", I salute Shiva and Parvati who are

the parents of the world and who are tied like word to its
meaning, have become legendary in Sanskrit semantics.
Kalidasa's *Kumarasambhava* remains the most evocative of the
various classical poetic works on Parvati. Written in faultless
classical Sanskrit it creates a lyrical image of Parvati, particularly
of her sensual beauty and romantic dalliance with Shiva, a work
that has not been surpassed. Kalidasa describes Parvati's beauty
thus:

> *Her youthful beauty was like a painting that unfolds under a*
> *painter's brush or the lotuses that bloom under the sun.*1.32
> *Her feet because of her painted toes gave to the earth the*
> *colour of red lotuses*
> *Her slender waist resembled an altar with three folds as if*
> *they were a flight of stairs for the God of love to*
> *ascend.* 1.33,39
> *Her breasts were so rounded that even a lotus fibre could not*
> *find space between them*
> *Her arms were more delicate than the* sirisha *flower*
> *Her sweet smile was comparable to a white flower on a tender*
> *leaf or a pearl resting on a coral*
> *Her voice was like music and her words like nectar*
> *Her flirtive glances were like the blue lotus tremulous in a*
> *strong wind*
> *Her long tresses put the deer to shame*
> *Indeed the creator had gathered all that was beautiful in her.*
> 1.41-49

While Kalidasa describes the wedding ceremony with great
finesse it is in the romantic dalliance of Parvati and Shiva that his
poetic skill is used to the fullest. The creation of a rich and
evocative sensuality without any trace of lewdness can only come
from the pen of Kalidasa. Here is how he describes those

wonderful romantic moments of Parvati in Kailasa:

Parvati became helpless when without her garments she closed Shiva's eyes with her two palms but Shiva continued looking with his third eye. 8.7

Although in the morning she was eager to tell her friends the erotic moments of the previous night she was too bashful. 8.10

And then after a few days Parvati, having tasted love, gradually gave up her shyness at the enjoyment of love sports. 8.13

She embraced her lover, did not turn away her face and did not obstruct his hand when it turned towards her garments. 8.14

In a few days their affection grew, they spent their time in pleasing gestures and conversation and they could not tolerate separation even for a moment. 8.15

It was Shiva who taught her romantic skills and she in turn taught him some more. This was her remuneration to her teacher. 8.17

When her lip was bitten she cooled it with the crescent moon on his head. 8.18

When Shiva's third eye was sore from the powder in Parvati's hair he held it to the breath of Parvati's mouth whose fragrance was like that of a lotus. 8.19

And thus Shiva lived by becoming a bee on the lotus of Parvati's mouth,on the slopes of Mandara where the stones were marked by the bracelet of Vishnu, where the breeze had blown through sandal trees and which wafted the fragrance of lavanga flowers, clasped by the tender arms of Parvati. 8.23-25

He enjoyed amorous sports being impassioned at seeing the face of his beloved Parvati, whose eyes were reddened owing to want of sleep, whose lower lip was injured owing to tooth

marks, whose hair was dishevelled and whose tilak *was*
wiped away. 8.88
Wishing to taste day and night, the nectar of the mouth of his
beloved, which enhanced his delight, he became invisible to
all who sought to see him. 8.90

A work of equal grace and charm by none other than Adi
Shankaracharya, the prince of Indian philosophers who
championed Advaita Vedanta, is *Saundaryalahari* a work
dedicated mainly to the celebration of Parvati's beauty. Even in a
single verse (97) he addresses her as queen of the supreme God,
goddess of learning, wife of the creator, goddess of riches,
daughter of the mountain, partner of the destroyer and a mystery
that dazzles the universe. Using the traditional *nakahshikha*
method of desricibing female beauty from the head to toe he
creates an exquisite and sensual picture of Parvati.

Daughter of the snowy mountains great poets like Brahma are
unable to describe your beauty. 12
You are the mind, you the ether, you are air, fire and water and
earth. You manifest yourself as the universe. 35
He who describes your golden crown studded with gem-like suns
would mistake the crescent moon as the bow of Indra. 42
Let the cluster of your hair soft and dense as the group of full blown
blue lotuses dispel our mental darkness. The flowers of trees in
Indra's garden have come to reside there. 43
The sindura *in the partition of your hair resembles the ray of the*
rising sun. 44
Your face puts to shame the radiance of the lotus with its gentle
smile, rows of beautiful teeth and fragrance. 45
Your eyebrows are like the bow of Cupid. 48
Your right eye is the sun and creates day, your left eye is the moon

and creates night. Your third eye radiant like the lotus creates
twilight. 48
Your elongated eyes are like the arrows of Cupid meant to disturb
Shiva. 52
Your eyes filled with compassion and adorned by red, white and
black create the three sacred rivers. 54
The learned have said that by closing and opening of your eyes the
universe is created and destroyed. 55
The bimba *fruit has derived its crimson colour by the reflection of*
your lips. 62
The chakora *birds drink moonlight which emanates from*
your smile. 63
The sweetness of your voice rivals that of the lute strings of
the goddess of sound. 66
Your neck resembles the stem of the lotus. 68
The beauty of your hands puts to shame the newly-open red
lotus at dawn. 71
Your breasts are jewelled chalices of nectar. 73
This thin line of hair above your slender waist looks lilke the
wave of the Yamuna river. 77
Place your feet on my head. The Upanishads *wear them like*
flowers, the Ganga waters them in worship and the radiance
of the red colour on them is that of the red ruby on the crown
of Vishnu. 84
The swans of your home imitate your beautiful gait. 91

Another poetic work eulogizing Parvati in all her glory is *Shri
Lalitastvaratnam* by Durvas. In ten verses (160-169) the poet paints
this beautiful picture of Parvati's beauty:
Ever do I remember the beautiful Parvati sitting on his lap,
shining like a foliage of the Kadamba
with her braid like a phase of the moon, with thick sindura *in*

her parting
her forehead shining with kumkum
a pearl ornament in her nose, smiling slightly
her lips outshining the bimba
her face covered with camphor paste
a pearl string hanging from her conch-like neck
creeper-like arms adorned with an armlet full of jewels
with pasa, ankusa, pundracapa *and* pushpastra *in her four hands*
high breasts, a line of creeper-like hair reaching up to her navel
with fleshy hips circumscribed by a girdle of rubies
her thighs like the trunk of elephants
her legs outstripping the victorious quiver of Kama
feet like the foliage of lotus.

Parvati's bashfulness is the subject of many a verse. Kalidasa's in *Kumarasambhava* (6.84) describes the scene when the sage Angirasa comes to the king of the Himalayas with the proposal that the king's daughter Parvati should be given in marriage to Shiva. When Parvati who was standing by her father's side, heard this "she bent her head and began to count the petals of a lotus". The phrase *"lilakamalpatrani ganayamas Parvati"* has become the standard illustration of *dhvani* or extended metaphor in Sanskrit criticism. At other times Parvati was able to hide her bashfullness and this is how Lakshimidhara describes it:

> *Whence comes this perspiration, love?*
> *From the fire of your eye*
> *Then why this trembling, fair faced one?*
> *I fear the serpent, prince*
> *But the thrill that rises on your flesh?*
> *Is from the Ganga's spray my lord*

May Gauri hiding thus her heart
for long be your protection.

It was common for Sanskrit poets to ask for Parvati's blessings but not without describing some aspect of her beauty. Notice how the poet Daksha does it:

May the toenails of the goddess
as Sthanu bows before them
protect the universe
The Ganga washes from their tips the red lac
which appears on his head-dress
as lovely as white jasmine buds
their flashing rays putting to shame the moon.

The poet Achalasimha asks for Parvati's protection thus:

Conspiring with the rays which dance
from Kama's fingernails across the curved hand
that plucks the bowstring
may Gauri's sidelong glance
graceful as a bee which darts to taste
the clustered buds that ornament her ear
be your protection.

And Bhasa invokes even the flowers that Parvati uses for worship:

As her wedding day approaches, Parvati
is told to worship God
but when she sees before her the image of her suitor
him who bears the Ganga
she hesitates with sentiments of rapture, laughter, anger and
then shame
And now I pray that those flowers which she finally offers to
her love

only with difficulty, by the older women bidden
may be for your protection.

The androgyn concept of the *ardhanarisvara* is central to Parvati's being but poets like Bhagiratha take the liberty of describing Shiva's predicament of being with Parvati in that state thus:
Lest the god's delight have been unsurpassed
that bearing your slender body joined to his
he receives, o Gauri, your tight embrace
still, Shiva's heart must often grieve
to think that your glance cannot by him be seen
sweet, loving and innocent and motionless with love.

The poet Mandana sees *ardhanarishvara* differently. Kartikeya is puzzled by half of Parvati residing in half of Shiva's body. He asks:
When father and mother became a single body
what happened elder brother to the other halves of each?
Victory to Ganesha, who explains to the young prince
The one on earth was born as everyman
the other every woman.

In a poetic work dedicated to Kamakshi titled *Panchashati*, Mahakavi Shri Muka eulogises her beauty in five hundred verses in five cantos thus:
O Kamakshi! Such is the charm of the dark lustre of your eyes
that it acted as the first sprout of smoke before the fire (that
shot forth from the third eye of Shiva)
the fire that burnt the crocodile-flagged god of love (Kama) to
ash
But the wonder of all wonders is that it generates joy in the
heart of the three-eyed god
the god with the mark of a deer in his crown. 1.37

*It is surprising that the quick movement of your flirtive eyes
which bring lustre to your face shake the firmness of Shambhu
and bind him to passion while they strengthen the bonds of
devotion in the sages.* 1.61

*O Kamakshi! Your gaze sprouts passion and desire and yet
fulfills the desires of your devotees. Although filled with
passion how is it that your eyes bespeak detachment to the
sages?* 1.70

*The black curls of your hair are flirting about your eyes,
bee-like*

*the rays from the pearl on your beautiful nose reveal a
sprouting bird*

*compassion O Mother! Is dripping from your eyes like honey
Therefore I should surmise that your look is no other than the
lotus itself.* 1.75

*O Kamaskshi! Your looks are drenched with the nectar of love
yet what a wonder that they, like firewood, kindle the fire of
lust in the heart of Kama's arch enemy.* 1.78

*O Kamakshi! Your gentle smile engenders the joy of filial love
in Ganesha and Kartikeya*

*it manifests in Shiva the arch enemy of Mara (Madana) the
germination of innate passion*

*in people who venerate you it inspires a complete
understanding of your compassion*

in what manner can I describe the blossom of your smile? 2.75

*O Kamakshi! May your lovely feet, consort of the divine dancer
with their jingling anklets and their soft and delicate
movements*

exhibit the lasya *dance on the stage of my heart
in harmony with* raga *and capturing the hearts of the
connoisseurs.* 3.90

I take refuge in the goddess of Kanchi who has beautiful and

seductive breasts, who has given herself up to Shiva, the
bearer of Ganga
and who is established in the doctrine of Shringaradvaita. 4.6
In Kanchi a young girl causes infatuation by the looks of her
eyes in the conqueror of Kama who wields five arrows. Her
eyes are indeed a great teacher of erotics. 4.9
Rendering dull by the lustre of your face the lotus arrow of the
love god, the fish flagged one
enfeebling the hamsa, *Brahma's vehicle, by the beauty of*
her gait
making the drink of the gods (nectar) distasteful by her
sweet words
this beautiful goddess with three eyes surveys the banks of the
Kampa river. 5.27

51

Banabhatta's classical Sanskrit play *Parvatiparinayam* describes
Parvati's marriage and the events leading upto it in dramatic and
evocative prose. A passage of exquisite beauty in that work is
when Narada journeys to Oshadhiprastha to meet Parvati's father.
Narada, writes Banabhatta, feels exhilarated as he rides the wind
like the pollen of the blossoming *nandana* flower and bees that
waft on perfumed wind. Looking underneath he sees the earth
where lofty peaks adorn the mountains and where clear streams
of water are to be seen, where trees steal the beauty of the clouds
and as he descends to earth from the sky it seems as if the trees
and creepers ascend upwards. The Himalaya mountain is truly
more magnificent than both the Mandara mountain and mount
Meru where fragrant trees grow. and is incomparable even to the
fourteen celestial worlds. Here the black deer lie content listening
to the music of the *kinnaras* and white deer are intoxicated with
the aroma of musk and having refereshed himself from the fatigue
of the journey Narada enters a fragrant path that takes him to

Oshadhiprastha. Here on the lofty and vast peaks of this mountain clouds come to rest and it is adorned by forests of wish-fulfilling trees and amidst this stands the palace where many gems have vitually created a rainbow.

Shiva and Parvati have been rightly called *adidampati,* the first couple, for much of the art and philosophy takes the form of a dialogue between the two. The 11th century Kashmiri author Somadeva's *Kathasaritasagara* begins with Parvati singing hymns of praise to Shiva in Kailasa. When Shiva asks her what makes her happy she asks for a story that is new and amusing and one that no one had heard before. After Shiva has narrated the story of her previous birth as the daughter of Daksha, Parvati is not satisfied and wants to hear more. At this point Shiva begins to tell her the tales of *vidyadharas.* And thus begins the *Kathasaritasagara* within the frame story of this dialogue of Shiva and Parvati. Each chapter of this book begins with an invocatory verse to Shiva and Parvati which also emphasises their romantic relationship:

May Shiva, the blue throated one, he who is ensnared by Parvati's noose-like glances, grant you prosperity.
May Shiva's sweat protect you, that water which is fresh from his embrace with Parvati and that is Kama's weapon against Shiva's fiery third eye.
The god of love conquers the world with his five arrows and Shiva trembles at his command when he is embraced by his beloved.
I worship the god of love whose arrows pierce even Shiva, making him bristle as if with thorns when he is in Parvati's embrace.
May Shiva's head protect you, marked on it by Parvati's nails as she playfully pulls his hair so that it appears studded with many moons.

The 16th century romantic text *Rasikapriya* by Keshav Das which portrays *nayikabheda* or the different types of romantic heroines begins with a prayer to Shiva and Parvati thus:

> Not to cause discomfort to Parvati, who is leaden with love that Shiva holds her to his left, sleeps to her right, plucks a flower from a tree with his right hand and extends his right foot forward. 1

The text while favouring Radha and Krishna as the romantic pair does not ignore the love of Shiva and Parvati.

> O lotus-eyed beauty! Who will be the fortunate one to make nail marks on your voluptuous breasts, as if to decorate Shiva's head of hair with the crescent moon? 6

> When Parvati saw her reflection in the moon on Shiva's forehead she mistook it for another lover dallying her with Lord. So in anger she raised her trembling hand adorned with sparkling bracelets to punish her Lord. 16

> Give back to me my necklace which you have stolen during our game of dice. Why do you deny that theft? I will not accept your words even though you carry the Ganga on your head, the fire you have in your eyes and the snakes you wear. These were the words of Parvati as she smiled. 97

> Seeing Parvati exhausted Shiva spoke thus: O moon! Drench her with your cooling waters. O snake, fan her with gentle breezes. O Ganga! Spread your cooling waters on the shirish-*like limbs of her who is oppressed by the heat of the sun.* 100

53

In the Tamil country early Shaivite literature was centred mainly around the godhead of Shiva, and Parvati was mentioned only in passing as his consort. While the Nayanmars or the Shaivite saints eulogised only Shiva it was left to the child-saint Sambandar to sing of the glory of Parvati. Sambandar's songs usually begin with the glory of Parvati and even when he wrote

of *ardhanarisvara* or the androgyn Shiva, he wrote of his left half
or Parvati thus:

She moves beautyfully like the swan
Like the kovai *fruit are her lips of scarlet hue*
Like pearls her shiny teeth
Beautiful Uma with wavy tresses is one half of the Lord of
Pundarai
where brahmins *equal in fame to the lotus born Brahma,*
worship the supreme Shiva
Come, let us too arise and go to Pundarai, let us bow to the
transcendent Lord.
Smooth and tortuous her stomach like the snake's
dancing hood
Her exquisite gait mocks the peacock's grace
With feet soft as cotton-down and waist a slender creeper
Uma devi is one half of Shiva, Lord of sacred Pundarai,
where grow the lotus and the water lily
Where live holy brahmins *chanting Vedic verses*
Come, let us too arise and go to Pundarai let us bow to the
transcendent Lord.
Fresh as nascent lotus buds, lustrous like kongu *blossoms,*
sweet like young coconuts
Golden kalashas *filled with the nectar of the gods are the*
breasts of resplendent Uma
She is part of the shining glory of Shiva of Pundarai
Where rare birds rest and fine flowers bloom in shaded
verdant groves
Come let us rise and go to Pundarai, let us bow at the feet of
the transcendent Lord.

It is only after the 16th century that Tamil poets began to glorify
the beauty and grace of Parvati. Parvati takes on a unique ethos

of her own in the hands of these poets and the literature takes the form of *sthalapurana*, place histories, where the persona and the deeds of Parvati are tied to a particular temple. A shining example of this is the 17th century work *Tiruvilaiyatrpuranam* or *Shiva's Sacred Games* by Paranjyoti which is considered the *sthalapurana* of Madurai. This work renders in beautiful verse the sixty-four exploits of Shiva in Madurai, but of these his marriage to the queen of Madurai called Tatatakai, later called Minakshi, is the most striking. From that work here are some excerpts describing how Parvati was adorned for the wedding:

> *Lakshmi the goddess of the red flower and Sarasvati the*
> *goddess of the white flower with their flower-like hands*
> *applied a red dye*
> *to her feet, feet so tender they fear to step on the delicate*
> *anicca flower*
> *Then they applied to her hair a fragrant ointment.* 156
> *On her swelling breasts they applied sandalwood paste mixed*
> *with cool rose water*
> *They placed on her feet beautiful red charming foot*
> *ornaments*
> *and dangling ankle-rings that sounded like noises made*
> *by swans*
> *whose red coral mouths open as they sit on lotus flowers.* 157
> *On her waist were five different kind of ornaments*
> *a thirty-two string waist band*
> *a jewelled girdle of twenty-one strands*
> *a belt of fourteen strings of beads and gems*
> *a beautiful strap made of eight strands*
> *and two belts of bells, each with seven strands*
> *that made noises like bees buzzing inside flowers.* 158
> *On her slender fingers, which looked like beautiful* kantal
> *flowers*

on which golden jewel-like bees had alighted
there were dazzling gold and blue sapphire rings
bracelets embedded with diamonds matched her red hands
and on her wide shoulders were armlets
all so brilliant that the sun in the sky seemd to bow down in
reverence. 159
A fragrant paste was smeared on her erect breasts
garlands of emeralds, lovely gold and coral
shone in rows like Indra's rainbow
and a garland of pearls resembled both the mountain
waterfall and its beautiful foam. 160
The large pearls she wore were like stars in the sky
surrounded by many jewels which were the planets
in one pendant she wore a large gem in the centre, it was like
the gleaming sun that makes darkness flee in fear
a pendant moving between her breasts was like the
constellation Ursa Major moving in an arc around mount
Meru. 161
With jewels given by the wish-granting tree they decorated
her body
to cause Shiva to gaze on our lady's beauty
to create everlasting joy and wonder in his mind
as they waited for the auspicious marriage hour. 164

The life and love of Parvati forms an important part of Tulsidas'
Ramcharitmanas. In Balkand, this is how he describes Parvati's
penance:

Cherishing in her heart the feet of her Lord, Uma went to the
forest and began her penance. Her delicate frame was hardly
fit for austerities, yet she renounced all luxuries and fixed her
mind on the feet of her Lord.

Her devotion to the feet of her Lord presented a new phase

everyday and she got so absorbed in penance that she lost all awareness of her body. For a thousand years she lived on roots and fruits alone, while for another hundred years she subsisted on vegetables. For some days her only sustenance was water and air, while for a few days she observed a rigorous fast. For three thousand years she maintained herself on the withered leaves of the Bela tree that fell to the ground. Finally she gave up even these dry leaves. Uma then came to be known as Aparna.

Seeing her body emaciated through self-mortification the deep voice of Brahma resounded through the heavens, "Listen O daughter of the mountain king, your desire is accomplished, cease all your rigorous penance, the slayer of Tripura will soon be yours." Balkand, 73, 1-4.

Many and varied are the folk songs of Parvati that are sung, usually by women. Spontaneous and simple, they revolve around the life and deeds of Parvati. The one episode in Parvati's life with which women generally associate themselves is her going away from her natal home to her Lord's home in Kailasa and this is a common theme of their songs. One of the songs sung by the women of Garhwal during the pilgrimage of Nandadevi goes as follows:

When young Gaura left, the drums began playing
Her conch and her bugles, they all began playing
Her brass plate and cymbals both began to play
Her mango wood palanquin covered with cloth with fringes of
pearls and a spinning parasol
The hour-glass shaped drum of the goddess was playing
The seven-mouthed conch of the goddess was playing
Beloved mother, please come dry my tears
Today I leave my loving parents' home
Maya Mainuli then grasped Gaura's hand

She grasped Gaura's hand, seated her on the palanquin
Maya Mainuli placed her hand on her head
Wherever you go girl, may you be happy
How can I leave this beautiful courtyard?
How can I leave this nine-pillared mansion?
How can I leave mother Mainuli's lap?
How can I leave my friends in the village?
How can I leave my elder brother's wife?

Modern poets have been equally touched by Parvati. The Nobel laureate Mexican poet Octavio Paz wrote:

At the top of the world
Shiva and Parvati caress.
Each caress lasts a century
For the god and for the man
An identical time.

In *Parvatidarpana* this is how I have described the mirror of Parvati:

Shiva's first cognition discovers the sensuous Parvati
but he cognises yet again and sees the mirror in her hand
The first cognition reveals the lustful Parvati
the second cognition none other than Shiva himself
in the mirror of Parvati.
Shiva is wonderstruck, he experiences the rasa of adbhuta
at the transformation brought about by the mirror
a movement from the enigmatic dvaita to the restful advaita
such is the wonder of pratyabhijna that creates the majestic advaita
not the advaita of negation but of affirmation, not where the mind whispers neti neti
but the chitta joyously exclaims iti iti.

And thus is Parvati celebrated in song and verse. Just as vocal music is the foundation of all other music and even dance in the Indian tradition, the literature of Parvati is the rich treasure of all of Parvati's images. It is in literature that she reveals herself in all her glory; it is in poetry that her *shringar* comes to life; it is in court drama that we can touch the intensity of her feelings; it is in devotional hymns that we can find the real aroma of her devotees and it is in the folk songs of the women that we see the human face of Parvati. It is literature that has inspired the varied and beautiful images and it is in this river of literature that we must dip again and again to understand and celebrate Parvati.

The Images of Parvati

A rt in India is never far removed from life, intimately tied as it is either to religion, aesthetics or utility. A portfolio of images, presented in this format is therefore out of context in many different ways. In the first place these images were never meant to be enjoyed as such. These images were part of a larger experience. Most of the stone images were part of a temple, usually the outer wall. Within the ambit of the temple the devotee gazed at these images during the *pradakshina*, circumambulation, and the images of Shiva and Parvati resonated with multiple others to provide the total experience. They were deeply meaningful only when visualised along with a universe of other images such as those of divine and semi-divine beings, cosmic manifestations, the world of animals and tress, mountains and rivers. They were seen, touched, loved, venerated and deeply felt, not just once but again and again, till they became a part of one's being. The bronze images came from the strong and sustained culture of temple images especially from the Chola period of Tamil Nadu. Most of them were festival images and seem singularly lonely in the present format, devoid as they are of throngs of faithful worshippers. The miniature paintings come from the courtly culture of the Himalayan kingdoms where they were enjoyed in elite company, often accompanied by the recitation of poetry. The folk images are part of festivals and rituals or the spontaneous earthy expression of ordinary people. The sensitive reader of this portfolio of images then is charged with the responsibility of

Parvati offering a drink to Shiva
1850, Jodhpur
Collection: Harsha Dehejia

On a terrace in Kailasa and behind a lotus pond it is time for an intimate repast. Seated on a tiger skin on a terrace and under the canopy of a tree it is time not only for a meal but equally to experience the pleasure and the joy of togetherness. Spread out in front of them on the terrace are two platters one of fruits and the other of drinks. Parvati affectionately offers a drink in a goblet to Shiva and Shiva in turn gladly accepts. Even though Parvati is involved in the process of feeding Shiva and both her hands are occupied she keeps her gaze steadfast on Shiva, for it is as important for her to quench his hunger and thirst as it is to receive and cherish his loving looks. While two owls keep a watch the peacock on the tree has turned his gaze upwards as if to invoke rain and the ever-faithful Nandi, richly decorated, stands guard at the foot of the painting. The Jodhpur *kalam* borrows a lot from the Kotah artists in creating iconic figures without losing the tenderness of feeling.

61

understanding and enjoying these images in their original context and not as mere art objects.

The pristine conceptions of Parvati are to be found not in plastic images but in the oral tradition, in the songs and stories of itinerant story tellers, and equally the dance dramas of a bygone era, a tradition that later evolved into the many structured *Puranas*. The *Puranas*, through the *kathas* and *gathas*, songs and stories, are the treasure-house of the Indian civilisation, and live not only through the many images they created but equally through the hands of *kirtankars* and *patua* singers, musicians and dancers who perform at fairs and festivals, in village squares and in temple precincts. An equally strong repository of the lore of Parvati is *natya,* dance dramas, where she comes alive in the gestures and movements of the dancer and in the lyrics and rhythm of the music. The literary arts, namely *sahitya*, have also eulogised Parvati, in many different ways. It is these ancient oral and literary artistic traditions that serve as the treasure house of the later manifold images of Parvati. The foundational source of the classical images of Parvati are therefore to be found in our literary and performing arts and it is to these that we must relate when we enjoy her visual and plastic images.

Our visual artists inspired by the rich oral and literary lore of Parvati have equally celebrated Parvati in stone and bronze, ivory and paper, and in a variety of styles. The visual expression of Parvati has depended not only on patronage and regional artistic styles but on the living presence of Shiva and Parvati in the artist's consciousness. The Indian artistic mind roams through vast vistas of creativity, where myth has a reality of its own, where the songs and stories of the tradition are never forgotten, where the immediate and the ultimate are a continuum; where colour is

not just a medium but a language, and line not just an outline but
the creation of a living space, where life pulsates through the
movement of breath and the pulsation of blood; where the shrubs
and the trees, blossoms and the birds are not just a part of the
landscape but an expression of the relationship between
humanity and nature, and where Shiva and Parvati are not deities
to be portrayed but to be realised in and beyond their artistic
manifestations. The images that follow are not cult images for
Parvati, unlike Durga or Kali, is not a cult goddess. These images
are primarily those of Shiva, but equally of his consort with whom
he dallies romantically in Kailasa; of his queen who presides in
his court, of his consort who also occupies half of his body, of the
mother of his two sons Ganesha and Kartikeya; of his family for
whom he is the provider and more than anything else of their
relationship which moves from the duality of love and romance to
oneness of ultimate realisation. Parvati can be seen, celebrated
and understood only through Shiva, in art as in thought.

The images in stone are mainly from the north and come from
what is called the classical period of Indian sculpture. The
dominant theme is the amorous togetherness of the divine couple,
and the images go by the generic term Uma-Maheshvara. Here
there is no story to be told, neither is there a representation of a
heroic act; it is not a manifestation of divinity, but a visual
testament of the romantic commitment as shown through their
loving embrace. In these images there is not only the romantic
submission of Parvati to her consort but equally the affectionate
embrace and acceptance by Shiva of her. In the tender
amorousness and the wistful gaze of this celestial couple there is
the bold expression of *shringara rasa*. And as witness to this
divine love there are not only the faithful Nandi but equally their
two children and celestial beings. The play of light and shade on

these images on the outside wall of a temple gives it a certain dimension of reality. In the mid-day sun there is a certain languidness about Parvati and under the moonlight one can see a romantic smile on her face. To the devotee who has just emerged from the temple and completed a *pradakshina*, there is a religious aura to these images. The togetherness of Shiva and Parvati creates the motif of biune unity, of two as in one, of Shiva and Shakti, and this then leads to the magnificent and ultimate vision of non-duality or *advaita*. And as devotees leave the temple and enter the secular world they are haunted by these images as they whisper to them of a love divine.

If the stone images from a temple create a religious aura, those from cave temples remind us of moments of deep learning and contemplation in the Indian tradition. These caves were primarily for monks who lived in them and the images on the walls were visual aids in their learning and meditation. Both the Kailasa temple in Ellora and the Elephanta caves near Mumbai, in their heyday, were inhabited by monks, who not only mastered the various Shaivite texts but took in the powerful visual experience generated by the panels in these caves in bas-relief. For these monks the arid metaphysical discourse was enlivened by these images, whether it was of Parvati holding Shiva's hand during the wedding ceremony or being comforted by Shiva when threatened by demons. These cave temples resonated not only with the chanting of the monks but equally with the visual presence of Parvati, one reinforcing the other.

Bronze as a medium of sculpture has been known in the Indian civilisation at least since 2500 BC, during the times of the Indus Valley. Bronze casting was known even in the south of India going back to the Satavahanas of the 2nd century AD. Metal work also flourished during the reign of the Pallavas, and Shankaracharya who lived in the 6th century AD and who was a contemporary of the Pallavas, gives the analogy of molten copper poured into a mould when he talks of the mind's capacity of perception. But it was not until the Cholas that some of the finest bronze sculptures were made. The lost-wax method of bronze casting that was used by the Chola artists has been described in texts of image-making of this period which also describe the five metals that go into the making of bronze, namely brass, copper, tin, gold and silver. The most renowned period of the Chola empire was the eleventh century, when two great emperors, Rajaraja and Rajendra, father and son, not only made their empire into a major political power but were responsible for the creation of the some of the most magnificent bronzes. These monarchs were considered the earthly manifestations of god and it is interesting to ponder the extent to which the artist identified god and the monarch in his creations. Another great patron of Chola bronzes was Queen Sembiyan Mahadevi who was widowed early in the reign of her husband king Gandaraditya and who devoted herself to temple art. Many of the depictions of Parvati during her period could easily be considered depictions of her rather than of Parvati. If stone sculptures bring to life the amorous togetherness of Shiva and Parvati in their celestial world, Chola bronzes give a plastic reality to the graceful and dignified contour of their bodies. Through their deflections, *bhangas,* the bronze images seem to possess a movement *in situ* even within their static framework. Parvati exudes both a divine grace and a regal majesty as she stands next to Shiva. The solitary Chola bronze images of the standing Parvati are a construct of modern museums, for she was never meant to stand alone apart from Shiva. Most of the Chola bronzes were *utsavmurtis* or festival icons which were ceremonially carried through the village, stopping at street corners and even at homes of devotees and then stored away in the temple till the next festival. The lugs on the base of the bronzes were meant for the insertion of poles which were then placed on the shoulders of the devotees who carried the image. The tradition of bronze sculptures was continued by the artists of the fifteenth century Vijayanagara kingdom and emperor Krishnadeva Raya was a great patron of the arts of this period. The Vijayanagar bronzes carry on the Chola tradition but introduced some stylistic changes of their own.

While bronze lent itself to the making of magnificent sculptures, ivory as a medium gave jewellers the opportunity to produce intricate and delicate images. Ivory was used not only for the making of objects of personal adornment but also for plaques and small images. Sixteenth and seventeenth century Madurai in Tamil Nadu and Pune in Maharashtra at a slightly later period were important centres for this type of art. Ivory carvers have a small but important place in Indian art. Bringing to their work the skill of jewellers they create small and delicate objects which are usually decorative rather than votive. While bronze and stone have life hidden in them, brought out by sculptors, ivory evokes a certain life of its own.

After the rout of the Vijayanagara empire by the confederacy of the Deccan sultanates, seventeenth and eighteenth century Thanjavur was to provide a refuge to artists of that kingdom. Thanjavur was then under Maratha rule and under the kingship of Shivaji and Sarbhoji. It was a time in the history of the subcontinent when Indian kings were selling themselves to their European colonisers and Thanjavur artists sought solace by creating iconic mythic images in their unique style. The decorative element was always more predominant than the iconic in this genre of painting. Ornate canopies, finely executed pillars and niches, chandeliers and furniture provide the ambience in which the figures were set. Thanjavur painting was generally done on jackwood which was pasted with unbleached cloth and to which a mixture of limestone, chalk powder, gum and honey was applied. The paintings were embellished with gold leaf and semi-precious stones. Although Thanjavur artists had a preference for Vaishnava themes they also represented Parvati in a variety of local temple traditions such as Shivakami at Chidambaram, Minakshi at Madurai and Kamakshi at Kanchi. Created mainly to adorn temple walls or home shrines, Thanjavur paintings with their brilliant reds and gold leaf encrustation created two-dimensional, richly resplendent, decorative icons. They were the last vestiges of traditional art before modern painting was to take over India.

While Thanjavur artists were creating their unique genre of paintings yet another chapter of Indian art was being written in the mountain kingdoms of the foothills of the Himalayas and in the princely states of Rajasthan, an art which was to portray Parvati in an inimitable idiom. These were the Pahadi and Rajasthani miniatures which, though partial to the Krishna lore, also took on the Shiva Parvati theme. In this genre of paintings, Parvati emerges as a dedicated wife, tending to Shiva's every need, being always by his side, assisting him in the making of *bhang*, Shiva's favourite intoxicant drink, in making a garland of skulls or sewing a quilt together in the idyllic surroundings of Kailasa. Parvati is also shown as the mother of her two children Ganesha and Kartikeya. The miniature artists portray Parvati in an attire typical of the region, set amidst the idyllic and picturesque landscape of Kailasa.

The patrons of the miniature paintings were Hindu kings and were establishing their political and cultural identity between the period of the decline of the Mughal empire and the establishment of the British raj. The technique of miniature painting had already reached a high watermark in the Mughal ateliers. The artists from those ateliers had migrated to Punjab and Rajasthan. Their new patrons, wishing to express their Hinduness, turned to traditional Hindu literature to express and celebrate their Hindu identity. Thus it is that the lore of Shiva and Parvati gave the impetus and inspiration to these artists to translate the life of this celestial pair into the beautiful idiom of miniature paintings. If stone sculptures gave Parvati a religious aura within the temple, the bronzes gave her an iconic presence in the Chola empire, the Thanjavur paintings added a decorative element, the miniature paintings gave Parvati a certain poetic truth. The paintings are indeed visual poetry. There is in these paintings an expression of both the romantic and the motherly love of Parvati, of her dedication to Shiva as his consort, of her graceful presence in the court of Sadashiva, of her femininity when she was being pursued by demons and of her joy when Shiva's needs are fulfilled. There is also in these miniature paintings, a feeling that despite his involvement in wordly affairs Shiva is ultimately a *yogi;* that despite his amorousness he ultimately prefers the solitariness of the snowy Kailasa; that even with the warm and effusive Parvati by his side he prefers to sit in cremation grounds and prepare his intoxicant. While the stone and bronze sculptures and the miniature paintings have a measured grace and refinement about them the folk representations of Parvati have a certain earthy charm and spontaneity. In her folk forms Parvati is not only more endearing but accessible, her presence is in the home shrine or the walls of the home. The Kalighat artists in Bengal or those of Madhuban in Bihar create folk images that may lack the sophistication and elegance of the classical representations but more than make up in their robustness and spontaneity. There is nothing plebeian or dull about these images, whether it be the calendar art of modern India which hangs in every village home, the creations of the village potter sold at fairs and bazaars or the scrolls of itinerant singers. Folk artists have the freedom of creating their own forms and of placing these forms in the composition without any *shastraic* injunctions. Thus in the *pichhwais* of Nathdwara, Shiva and Parvati are shown as flying celestial figures blessing a Vaishnava celebration, while in a scroll of Gujarat they adorn the top of the composition. The narrative in such scrolls is oral rather than painted as the narrator keeps his audience spellbound by the various stories that he spins. As the narrator regales the assembled gathering Parvati assumes a reality in their minds. These are not icons for contemplation, nor are they visual poetry, but mythic beings reduced to everyday reality. The folk Parvati is one that the common person can relate to, worship and celebrate in his or her own personal way. The driving and motivating force of folk artists, many of them women, is a joyous expression of the womanhood of Parvati rather than the creation of icons in keeping with the canons of image-making. Calendar or bazaar art owes its inspiration to Raja Ravi Verma, the nineteenth century painter from Kerala who created portraits of mythic images using Western techniques. These creations, though not universally acclaimed, found instant and widespread acceptance at the popular level, and once they were mass produced through the printing press, were hung in every village hut and urban tenement. Parvati in these forms of bazaar art was easily accessible to the masses.

Uma-Maheshvara
8th century, sandstone
Gujarat
Collection: Dayton Art Institute

While this composition
follows the general pattern of
such images one cannot miss
the smiles on the rounded
faces of Shiva and Parvati as
they are locked in an
affectionate embrace. While
he drapes his upper left hand
over Parvati's left shoulder his
lower right hand is poised to
caress her. Shiva's crown of
matted hair holds a snake
while a celestial figure stands
behind Parvati's coiffure. The
base of the composition is full
of figures highlighted by a four
armed Ganesha who balances
the emaciated figure of
Bhringi, a devotee of Shiva,
while Kartikeya astride his
peacock appears by the
goddess's foot. On either side
stand guardian figures. While
this piece bears some
resemblance to the sculptural
style of Gujarat it conforms
more to the compositions of
Madhyadesh or the area
around the Ganga-Jumna
valley near Kanauj.

Uma-Maheshvara

11th century, Pala

Collection: Harsha Dehejia

This Uma-Maheshvara image executed in the typical Pala style in black stone is as intimate as it is eloquent. The most arresting part of the composition is Shiva's gentle touching of Parvati's face drawing it romantically towards him. The gesture speaks clearly of his need for her affection. In responding to this gesture Parvati affectionately draws herself near. The ambience is immediately one of animated conversation between the two. The limbs, done in slender outline in keeping with the Pala style, rest on Nandi and a lion which provide stability to the composition. The background is uncharacteristically bare and devoid of the usual Pala adornments but is marked by Shiva's hand holding aloft the trident.

71

Ardhanarishvara
6th century, Elephanta Caves, Maharashtra

This majestic relief from the 6th century cave-temple at Elephanta near Mumbai is not merely a relief sculpture but an epiphany. The assembly of gods and goddesses celebrate the biune unity of Shiva and Parvati as *ardhanarishvara*. The *tribhanga* icon leans easily on Nandi and its four arms keep the rushing assembly at bay. Parvati holds a mirror in her upper hand while the lower reaches downward. The bottom of the composition is made up of Kartikeya on the right and Jaya Vijaya on the left. Brahma sitting on a lotus and Indra on Airavata are on the right while Vishnu riding his *garuda*, eagle, is on the left.

Flying celestial figures make up the top of the relief. The figures appear as if emerging from the unhewn rock and become manifest suggesting the *vyaktavyakta*, manifest-unmanifest state of Shiva. The serene expression on the face of the *ardhanarishvara* stems from the joyous realisation of the dynamic harmony of Shiva and Parvati.

Ardhanarishvara
10th century, sandstone
Uttar Pradesh
Collection: Harsha Dehejia

In this strikingly beautiful androgyn image there is a dynamic harmony between Shiva on the right side and Parvati on the left. While blending into biune unity both Shiva and Parvati maintain their independent identity and appearance. While Shiva's hair is matted, Parvati's is flowing; Shiva's limbs have masculine strength while Parvati's show feminine grace. Shiva holds the *akshmala*, beads, in one hand and the *trishul*, trident, in the other. Paravati holds the *kalasha*, pot, in one hand and a mirror in the other. The bottom of the relief is adorned by two devotees. The expression of the biune image is one of serenity born of realisation. There is a suggestion of arrested movement in the stunningly expressive half-Shiva and half-Parvati composition, suggested not only by the *tribhanga*, thrice broken pose, but equally by the inherent movement in the coming together of Parvati and her lord, the togetherness of female and male, the oneness of *prakriti* and *purusha*, the unity of the primal object and subject.

73

Shiva and Parvati

6th century, beige sandstone
Madhya Pradesh
*Collection: National Gallery of
Canada, Ottawa*

In this early sculpture, cut off
from its base, Parvati sits on
Shiva's vast left thigh in the
pralambapadasana pose with
pendent legs. Shiva embraces
her with his left hand which
rests on her left shoulder.
Parvati holds her left hand in
katakamukha mudra while the
right hand is held in *suchihasta*
as an expression of her
coyness at her lord's embrace.
Shiva offers his grace to her by
resting his right hand in the
varadamudra on his right knee.
In his second right hand he
holds a rosary of *rudraksha*.
Parvati's hair is made up into a
chignon and she sports a
single earring in her left ear.
Shiva's jewellery is more
dominant and his clothes are
shown by ripples on his leg.
Shiva's hipband is dominated
by his erect phallus which
along with his embrace
indicates his erotic mood;
however the enigmatic smile
on his face tempers any
tension this may create. The
mood of the composition is
one of unhurried amorousness
and brings out the romantic
relationship of this divine
couple.

Ravana Shaking Mount Kailasa
9th century, sandstone
Rajasthan
Collection: Eugene Fuller Memorial Collection, Seattle Art Museum
Photograph: Paul Macapia

In this composition from the exterior wall of a temple in north-eastern Rajasthan, Parvati does not hide her fear as she is shown seeking shelter from Shiva during one of the many episodes in Kailasa when she was threatened by a demon. When Ravana, King of Lanka, was denied permission to enter Kailasa, where Shiva and Parvati were dallying, he was enraged, grabbed the mountain and shook it. Shiva only had to press his right toe to make it steady. Parvati in clasping Shiva's chest expresses her trepidation at the shaking of the mountain but equally derives strength and support from her lord as he presides on the throne, while their two children, Ganesha and Kartikeya are at their side. The narrative is framed between pilasters with foliate capitals. The many-armed Ravana is finally subdued and Parvati is relieved of her fear. In seeking shelter and protection from Shiva, the artist has been able to depict visually Parvati's love and dependence on him.

Wedding of Shiva and Parvati

7th – 9th century AD
Black stone
Kailasa Temple, Ellora Caves
Maharashtra

In this grand monolithic temple dedicated to Shiva and Parvati at Ellora the presence of this divine couple is felt in every stone. The corridor around the shrine is replete with images of Shiva and Parvati depicting the many events in their lives but the centre of attention is the moment in the wedding ceremony when Parvati's hand is held by Shiva as the union is being solemnised by Brahma who is not in this picture. This moment is the culmination of Parvati's *tapasya* and her expression, one of restrained joy and the shy expectation of a bride, speaks a thousand words. Shiva's towering presence besides her cannot hide his feeling of romantic excitement. Both bride and groom are adorned with exquisite jewellery. The otherwise bare panel leaves the viewer imagining the charged atmosphere at this august event where gods and goddesses, kings and queens and the entire town of Aushidaprastha had gathered.

Utsavmurti of Queen Sembiyan Mahadevi as Parvati

10th century, Chola bronze
Tamil Nadu
*Collection: Freer Gallery,
Washington, D.C.*

Even though goddesses were portrayed as early as the Indus Valley civilisation it was left to the Chola artists of the 10 and 11th century Tamil Nadu to create a form that could contain the greatness and grandeur, the majesty and beauty of the goddess as Parvati. They fashioned a Parvati that was at once sensuous and serene, regal and splendorous. Using traditional *bhangas* or deflections, *mudras* or gestures, jewellery and costumes, they created an icon of a goddess that has never been surpassed. While the *bhangas* give a sense of movement, the *hastamudras* add grace and the crown gives Parvati a regal dignity that shines through her serene expression. The opulence of the female body is used at its best to express feminine charm and divinity in the same form. While the well-endowed breasts and rounded hips suggest fertility, the crowning *jatamukuta* leaves no doubt that Parvati is both

queen and goddess at the same time. The legs and hips, bejewelled and draped, give both stability and movement to this standing figure. The solitary standing Parvati is in many ways a modern museum construct for in her natural environment she would almost always stand next to Shiva. The bronze Parvati is an *utsavamurti* that was taken out ceremonially on certain occasions and later stored in the temple. Parvati, serene and self-enchanted, is so charged with beauty that she animates the space around her and sends vibrations in all directions. The standing bronze Parvati is the finest example of a perfect female form in the Indian tradition, a form that has not been surpassed, and remains an anthropomorphic perfection, inviting the sensitive onlooker to go beyond the form to the formless spirit of the great goddess.

77

Somaskandamurti
11th century, Chola bronze
Tamil Nadu
*Photograph: Sotheby's
New York, 1997*

The inspiration for this Chola Somaskandamurti comes from the 7th century rock-cut Pallava sanctuaries which show Parvati with Shiva and their son Skanda. The composition is an exegesis of Shiva in his aniconic *linga* form and is a precursor of the holy family depicted by the later Pahadi artists. Shiva and Parvati are both seated at ease in the *lalitasana* pose with one leg bent and the other pendent. Shiva's right hands are in the *katakamudra* and *abhaya mudra* while the left would be holding a battle axe and the antelope. Shiva is dressed in a short *dhoti* and wears armbands and bracelets and his hair is arranged in a tall *jatamukuta*. Parvati holds a lotus in her right hand and the left is kept in *dhyanamudra,* meditative gesture. Her jewellery is arranged in a tiered conical *karandamukuta*. Skanda is in a *tribhanga*, thrice-broken pose, and stands between the two. While Shiva's serenity and power are obvious he does not hide the fact that his strength is derived from Parvati. Not only does he wear a large *kundala* in his left ear which depicts his feminine aspect but he sits so that Parvati is never out of his sight. Parvati's smile indicates that she cannot hide her pleasure at being with her Lord and son and this leads to a contemplative self-realisation as seen by her left hand. Parvati's presence in this significant Chola composition is both maternal and spiritual.

Kalyanasundara Parvati
10th century, Chola bronze
Tamil Nadu
*Collection: Thanjavur Art
Gallery*

The Chola artist has captured
the excitement and
anticipation of Parvati as a
bride as she holds Shiva's
hand. It is a charged moment
as it is the culmination of her
tapasya, as she takes her place
rightfully as Shiva's *vama*
before the assembled guests.
In her expression is the self-
assurance of her love and the
pride of belonging to Shiva.
The deflection of her body
towards Shiva indicates that
while offering her very being
to Shiva she will still stand
with grace and dignity besides
him. This is the true standing
Parvati for she stands firm but
besides him who is her Lord.

80

Umasahita Chandrashekharamurti
11th century, Chola bronze
Tamil Nadu
*Collection: British Museum
London*

The double *alingan*, embrace, in this early Chola bronze beautifully demonstrates visually the togetherness of Shiva and Parvati. Standing tall with a towering crown Shiva embraces her with an arm that provides comfort and protection to Parvati and with his other blesses with the *abhayamudra*. Parvati not only accepts this gesture but in turn converts it into a romantic moment by embracing Shiva in turn. It is the left shoulder of Parvati that provides the nexus to this image for it is at that point that the various forces resolve. In accepting the embrace she turns slightly and affectionately towards him. Shiva and Parvati stand on a common pedestal but the slight rotation of Shiva's left foot towards Parvati indicates that it is she who is the centre of his attention.

Wedding of Shiva and Parvati

17th century, Ivory, Madurai, Tamil Nadu
Collection: Victoria and Albert Museum, London

The Minakshi temple in Madurai fostered a number of arts, one of which was ivory carving. Ivory carvers were usually jewellers who were able to do fine and intricate work. The nature of ivory permits only small creations such as this panel which was probably nailed to a wooden background. In this panel the artist has not only been able to include all the main figures present at Parvati's wedding but has created a work of great delicacy. Under a foliate canopy a demure Parvati offers her right hand to Shiva, while Vishnu and Lakshmi stand affectionately behind her. The artist has paid special attention to the jewellery on all the four figures leaving no doubt that he was a jeweller. It is an important moment for Parvati as she looks at Shiva's hand with anticipation and expectation while Shiva is unable to hide his pleasure.

Uma-Maheshvara
1750, Ivory, Maharashtra
Collection: Harsha Dehejia

Carved into the tusk of a
mature elephant this sculpture
makes a strong iconic impact.
Created either to decorate a
niche in a court or *haveli* the
artist captures the
togetherness of Shiva and
Parvati with a special
tenderness given only to ivory
carvers. Parvati, wth a
pendent arm that probably
held a mirror, sits on Shiva's
broad thigh while Shiva holds
his hand in *abhaya mudra*.
The divine couple are self-
absorbed and contemplative
not about their own state but
that of the world of which they
are the parents. They have put
away their romance for the
time being while they care for
the world around them. The
workmanship of this sculpture
is in contrast to the delicate
work of the Madurai panel.

83

The Shiva Family descending from Kailasa

19th century, Western Punjab Hills

Lent by Shubhash Kapoor, Art of the Past, New York

It is a commonly held belief by those who dwell in the Himalayas that Shiva Parvati and their retinue descend from their abode in Kailasa and come down to earth to care for all of their creation. Here the holy family negotiates a cobbled pathway in the Kailasa mountain. The leader of the pack is Nandishvara the monkey-shaped *gana* who carries a *mridanga* on his shoulder and a bundle of Shiva's meagre belongings on his head. Shiva is dressed in a leopard skin skirt, a matching hat and a scarf of tiger skin and affectionately helps Parvati, holding baby Kartikeya, to climb down from a rock. In the rear Parvati's tiger is followed by Shiva's Nandi with Ganesha and a peacock riding on it, and Ganesha's rat. This is not merely a visual record of Parvati's journey, but an affirmation that she participates fully in Shiva's responsibilities. There is no sparkle of romance or a suggestion of play in this composition. Instead there is in every face, including those of the animals, an honest determination to fulfill one's duty. This is an event in Parvati's life, marked by work and a fulfilment of her duty, for she knows that she is not only Shiva's consort and the mother of his two children but the mother of all that he creates.

Ardhanarisvara
18th century, Kotah
Collection: Harsha Dehejia

Standing on a lotus pad this figure of the *ardhanarisvara* dominates the space which is otherwise bare. The golden Parvati in her red flowing sari holds a lotus and is flanked by a lion. The blue Shiva in a golden *dhoti* holds the trident and carries Ganga on his head. He is flanked by Nandi who receives the waters of the Ganga. The two halves are held in perfect balance not only by their proportional representation but by the harmony of colours. The artist, in depicting Parvati's lion in Shiva's garment stresses this harmony and the inter-dependence of the two. The Kotah *kalam* that relies on strong outlines creates an icon of this androgyn image of Shiva and Parvati, that stand with certitude and expresses not only their togetherness but their strength in biune unity.

Shiva and Parvati in a grove

19th century, Kangra
Collection: Harsha Dehejia

Kangra artists who had a penchant for depicting the lore of Radha and Krishna use their well honed artistic idioms and almost succeed in tricking the viewer into believing that this is another painting of Radha and Krishna. This delightful composition is actually that of Shiva and Parvati in a grove. A stylised grove with red blossoms creates a space where Shiva and Parvati sit on a canopied throne enchanted with each other's company. The strength of the composition is the locked gaze as Shiva turns affectionately towards Parvati and Parvati holds up her hand in adoration. It is a moment of total devotion and dedication, a culmination of her *tapasya* or austerities, the crowning event of their amorous togetherness. The mood is one of romantic anticipation and the air seems to be filled with the aroma of the blossoms. The otherwise scantily clad Shiva is in a regal attire with a bejewelled crown, bracelets, armbands, earings and necklace. In his right hand he holds a noose and with his left an *ankush* or goad as he rests this arm on Parvati's leg in an expression of tender affection. Shiva wears a richly decorated red *dhoti*. While the Ganga is missing from his head the crescent moon is the only give away of Shiva's usual adornments. Parvati by comparison is more sedately attired and her long and flowing hair is covered by a diaphanous *odhni*. The ornate hexagonal throne provides a resting point for a moment of romantic togetherness. And as our attention turns away one cannot help but compare for a moment this charmed moment with the dalliance of Radha and Krishna.

Raga Bhairavi

18th century, Deccan
Collection: Harsha Dehejia

This 17th century Deccani Ragamala painting creates an unusual ambience of a Shiva shrine within a *haveli* in the vicinity of a mosque by a lake. Parvati, with three of her *sakhis*, offers worship to the aniconic Shiva. The jars in the hand of the *sakhi* and by the knee of Parvati, as also the fountain at the bottom of the painting and the bell without a proper temple background suggest that Parvati is not in Kailasa but in a courtly environment to which she will return after the worship is over. While one *sakhi* sprinkles rose water and reassures Parvati with her right hand, the second *sakhi* looks longingly and the third draws strength from the sight of Nandi. Flowers are important in this painting as they appear as lotuses in the lake, roses by the fountain and also on the *linga*. Ragamala artists, and particularly those of the Deccan, took the liberty of mixing both a Hindu and a Muslim ethos in creating a visual picture of a *raga* as we see in this painting. A picture such as this draws its inspiration from music texts such as *Sangita Sara Sangraha* rather than mythic literature. The rounded faces of the women suggest a Kotah influence on this Deccani artist.

Shiva and Parvati playing Chaupat
17th century, Basohli
Collection: Metropolitan Museum of Art, New York Gift of Dr J. C. Burnett

It is a charged moment in the game of *chaupat* that Shiva and Parvati have engaged in at the behest of Narada. Shiva loses in the game and agitation is writ large on his face as he steals Parvati's necklace. Seated across him and on a tiger skin is Parvati who, with her uplifted left hand protests at Shiva's behaviour, and stares at him. She hides her anger just as she conceals the tiger claws behind her back. The stylised trees offer a canopy to Parvati indicating that the world around favours Parvati in this tussle with the mighty Shiva.

Yellow is the dominant colour broken only by the green of the trees and the red of Parvati's garments and the *chaupat*. The brilliant colouration and the bold figures are in keeping with the Basohli style although the typical Basohli foliage is not present in this painting.

The Penance of Parvati
19th century, Rajasthan
Collection: Baroda Museum and Picture Gallery

This painting tells the story of the penance and the marriage of Parvati. The top right of the composition shows her mansion where, in the presence of her parents and courtiers, she embarks on her austerity to win the heart of Shiva. Her parents bless her though with a heavy heart, and Mena, her mother cries "O ma". Dressed as a *sanyasini* in a garment of leaves, the four-armed Parvati is shown carrying a *linga*, Ganesha, a *mala* and a pot in her hands. Shiva, in the guise of a tall *sanyasi*, appears in the bottom of the composition and is approached by a *sakhi* who explains the reason for Parvati's penance. The *sanyasi* castigates Shiva, remarks which Parvati refuses to listen and to believe; she plugs her ears. Shiva, having satisfied himself about Parvati's sincerity reveals himself and is shown in animated conversation with Parvati. The composition is divided by stylised trees and mountain ranges of Kailasa. The artist has skilfully managed to depict a narrative without sacrificing the visual beauty of the environment.

Shiva and Paravti in Kailasa

18th century, Chamba
Collection: National Gallery of Canada, Ottawa

It is an idyllic Kailasa with blossoming trees and the flowing Ganga. In their midst Parvati prostrates herself to Shiva. As she holds his feet Shiva lovingly touches her hand and in that moment there is a tender acceptance of Parvati's love. Witness to this charming event are their two children Ganesha and Kartikeya but equally Nandi whose eyes are always turned towards his master. Parvati's tiger engages a demon. The chill of Kailasa is more than recompensed by the log fire but more importantly by the loving togetherness of the family. In submitting herself to Shiva, Parvati is aware that she is not alone in Kailasa and the artist makes that point by inhabiting the space around them by a microcosm of Shiva's family, including their children, trees and animals. Parvati's red skirt indicates her passion, matched by the *dhoti* of the demon who lusts for her.

91

Parvati preparing *bhang* for Shiva

18th century, Guler
Collection: Harsha Dehejia

The preparation and the enjoyment of *bhang*, a liquid intoxicant drink favourite of Shiva, is an important activity in which Shiva and Parvati participate equally. Seated on a leopard skin which blends with Parvati's skirt, the ashen Shiva wears a loincloth and is adorned sparingly by a necklace, armband, bracelet, and by his snake which also partakes of *bhang*. The ambience of a cremation ground is created by the skull and burning logs. The bejewelled and demure Parvati seems totally involved with serving *bhang* from a terracota pot and is surrounded by ingredients and utensils needed for making the drink. Parvati seems as if she not only offers Shiva the drink but equally herself. Providing a canopy above Shiva's matted hair is a tree with fine foliage done in the typical Guler style. Although the *trishul* is missing from the composition the trunk of the tree seems to suggest a pillar. The amber background above the low hills infuses a languid afternoon mood. The Guler artist frames his beautiful composition in an oval floral frame.

92

Parvati with Sadashiva
19th century, Kangra
Collection: Harsha Dehejia

This regal composition shows Parvati as a queen in the court of the five-faced, ten-armed Sadashiva. The centre of our attention is drawn to the golden throne where Shiva majestically presides, not in his usual ashen body and loin cloth but in a golden *dhoti*. Shiva holds a fan, sword and *trishul* in his right hands and a drum, snake and an *ankush*, goad, in his left hands. The bejewelled Parvati sits regally to Shiva's left with an expression that befits a queen. The aristocratic ambience of the court is dominated by Shiva's sons Kartikeya on the right, and Ganesha on the left, with a host of musicians, *kinnaras* and a couple of mendicants. In the foreground two dancers complete the court scene. The backdrop of the composition is made up by the lush foliage of trees. Sadashiva is not only the cynosure of attention in this courtly composition but equally of adoration and worship. The viewer wishing to adore Shiva quickly identifies with the adoring Parvati.

Shiva dancing before Parvati

19th century, Mandi
Lent by Shubhash Kapoor, Art of the Past, New York

Shiva dances a thousand dances for he expresses his very being through his dance. Kailasa has become an auditorium for Shiva's *ananda tandava* or dance of bliss and presiding on the throne is Parvati. Gathered at the periphery are an august assembly. This includes Brahma and Vishnu, Ganesha and Kartikeya, gods and goddesses, men and women, kings and queens and *kinnaras,* each of whom contributes to the dance recital. While most of the assembled provide a beat to the dance with their hands, Narada plays the *ektara,* others a bugle, a monkey faced *kinnara* plays the *mrindangam* and celestial musicians play the trumpet. The dance is dedicated to Parvati, who is here not just as a consort but as a goddess, a four-armed *devi,* sitting in regal dignity, holding a *trishul* on a canopied throne. Her *sakhis* behind her hold a *chauri* and a fan. Within the intimate audience the space is charged with Shiva's dance which is meant as an offering

to Parvati and she in turn accepts it through the *varadamudra* of her lower right hand. Next to Parvati's wedding this is one event where all of Kailasa join in the celebration.

94

Parvati being pursued by a Demon

17th century, *Shiv Purana*
Lent by Shubhash Kapoor, Art
of the Past, New York

In this scene from the *Shiva
Purana* Jalandhara, a
ferocious demon, persues a
frightened Parvati as both
Shiva and Nandi rush to her
rescue. The horrific Jalandhara
with menacing teeth, large
ears and a hairy body holds a
discus which he wishes to use
as a missile to capture the
beautiful Parvati. The bare
chested Shiva carries his
trishul and drum in his right
hand but with his left reaches
out to Parvati to protect her.
While getting closer to Parvati
Shiva keeps an eye on the
demon while the faithful
Nandi hurries towards her. It
is a rocky Kailasa with sparse
vegetation in keeping with the
tension of the situation. The
artist succeeds in capturing
everyone in motion and with it
carries our attention and our
heart to the fleeing and
vulnerable Parvati as we wish
for her safety.

The Shiva Family
18th century, Bundi
Collection: Harsha Dehejia

It is a moment of worship and contemplation in Kailasa. Parvati, with folded hands leads the way in offering adoration to the contemplative Shiva. Shiva having seen Parvati through the corner of his eyes turns his body towards her. The two *chauri* bearers are their two sons Ganesha and Kartikeya. In addition Ganesha holds a leaf from a manuscript and this adds an air of piety to the occasion. Ganga takes the form of a face that emerges from Shiva's crown and the waters of the river flow from her mouth. As Parvati holds her hands in adoration she receives a stream of water from the tree above which makes that tree a *kalpavriksha* or a wish fulfilling tree. This *kalpavriksha* also provides a canopy for Shiva. Between Shiva and Parvati the artist places a stylised Kailasa in the shape of a tree on top of which is their mansion. The bottom of the composition is made up of Parvati's tiger and Shiva's Nandi. Shiva carries two necklaces around his neck, one of human skulls and the other of *rudraksha* beads. Parvati is dressed in her usual

red skirt. The tree plays an important part in most paintings of Shiva and Parvati; however the Bundi artist in this case, in depicting the *kalpavriksha* and placing the mansion on a stylised Kailasa makes the tree into a shrine and imparts a certain sanctity to the ambience.

Parvati as Annapoorna
18th century, Kangra
Collection: Harsha Dehejia

Seated on a lotus on a
canopied throne Parvati, in
her form as Annapoorna,
receives a mendicant Shiva
who approaches her with an
empty bowl. In one had

Parvati holds a ladle and in
the other a *kalasha*, pot, while
a number of vessels lie at the
foot of the throne. Dressed in
her regal red attire and
wearing a crown Parvati
assumes the form of a goddess
and is the provider rather than
a consort. Shiva in his
bhikshatana form receives the

offering with gratitude. The
landscape is bare except for
two trees, and the yellow
background contrasts with the
pallor of the terrace. Parvati's
expression is one of loving
adoration of one who seeks
alms and Shiva in seeking
alms shows the joy of a higher
realisation.

Shiva's Family
1840, Guler
Collection: Harsha Dehejia

This Guler artist captures the starkness of a cremation ground along with idyllic surroundings in this beautiful moment in the life of Shiva's family. While the ashen Shiva is the centre of the composition, he turns his head towards Parvati and in doing so makes her the focus of our attention. Draped in a red garment with Kartikeya on her knee, Parvati is both mother and consort, expressing maternal concern with her left hand and sheer joy with her right. She is firmly established on a leopard skin but has a dreamy far away look in her eyes. Shiva assists Ganesha and Kartikeya in the making of a garland of skulls. The ever-faithful Nandi provides the backdrop and easily overshadows the jackals at the bottom of the composition. The trident with the drum behind Ganesha has a stronger presence than the lush green tree on which is perched a peacock and from which hangs Shiva's bag. Large boulders, bones and a river make up the bottom of the composition while rolling hills take the eye to the horizon.

The Shiva Family

1810, Kangra
Collection: Basant Kumar Birla, Calcutta

The Kangra artist converts Kailasa into a tryst for the Shiva family. The preparation of *bhang* has brought together the loving family. Kartikeya has gathered the leaves, Ganesha works the mortar, Parvati holds up the muslin cloth and Shiva filters the drink. While the family is engrossed their animals rest; while Nandi, the lion and the rat are together at the bottom of the composition the peacock perches on a tree. Shiva and Parvati sit on an elephant hide. The doe-shaped eyes of Parvati, a characteristic of the Kangra *kalam*, though turned in, convey a certain peace and love that binds this holy family, of which she is, in many ways, the reason and the nucleus.

Uma-Maheshvara
19th century, Thanjavur
Tamil Nadu
Collection: Harsha Dehejia

The Thanjavur artist catches
Shiva and Parvati together on
a Nandi in a processional
event. Carrying a flag and a
chauri in front and a *chatri*
and emblem behind, Shiva's
ganas flank the graceful Nandi
which has become a throne for
Shiva and Parvati. Parvati,
seated on his thigh, is
affectionately held by Shiva
with his left hand while he
displays the antelope and the
battle axe with his other
hands. His main right hand is
in the *abhaya mudra*. The
group of devotees at the
bottom of the composition is
led by the three-legged
Bhringi. This is a public
moment and in keeping with
the occasion Shiva has a
patriarchal smile and Parvati a
restrained presence.
Processions are an important
part of the temple culture of
Tamil Nadu and the
Thanjavur artist captures that
ambience with gold crusting,
coloured stones and ornate
decoration set against a regal
red background.

Parvati as Shiva Kami
19th century, Thanjavur
Tamil Nadu
Collection: Harsha Dehejia

This is a recreation by the
Thanjavur artist of the temple
at Chidambaram. Shiva as
Nataraja presides in the
central shrine, Parvati is in the
shrine to the left, while the
rest of the space in the temple
is occupied by devotees
including the three-legged
Bhringi. Parvati's presence is
iconic. Holding a garland in
her pendent left arm she holds
a flower in her right and her
green body and sumptuous
attire gives her the aura of a
queen. The artist uses the
Thanjavur trademark gold leaf
decoration to advantage in
creating the *gopuram* and
pillars of the temple. The
atmosphere is distinctly
devotional as we are drawn
along with the retinue of
devotees in offering our
worship to Parvati.

101

**Shiva and Parvati as
Celestial Figures**
From a 19th century
Nathadwara *pichhwai*
Collection: *Harsha Dehejia*

Shiva, Parvati and Ganesha
Jamini Roy, 19th century
Photograph: Sotheby's, 1997

Shiva and Parvati
Popular Art

Shiva and Parvati
19th century, Patna
Collection: Harsha Dehejia

Nandadevi
Collection: Prof. William Sax
New Zealand

Parvati with Ganesha
Bastar, Madhya Pradesh
Early 20th century
Collection: Harsha Dehejia

Gangaur
Photograph: Dinodia Picture
Agency, Mumbai

Khandoba
19th century, Maharashtra
Collection: Harsha Dehejia

The Meanings of Parvati

After dipping ourselves in the life and the loves of Parvati through various myths, celebrating her many forms and manifestations, indulging in her poetic as well as plastic images we cannot take leave of her unless we have understood who Parvati really is, what she stands for and what is the *artha* or meanings of this multifaceted, multidimensional, radiant goddess of love. We cannot be mere voyeurs in her romantic dalliance. We must be philosophers of the arts and our quest should be *artha*, for that is the central concern of the philosopher. It is not enough to let ourselves be stimulateud by a superficial, sensual, cursory art-encounter with her. Parvati would not let us. Ours is a mythopoeic tradition where symbols and stories, icons and ideas are not only for our immediate attention but must be probed and carried to its ultimate, full, rich and intuitive understanding.We must pick up the various hints and suggestions and penetrate the layers of meanings that they prompt, like a needle that goes through a pile of lotus leaves. Parvati is not just an icon to be worshipped, an art object to be curated in a museum, a symbol to be decoded, a metaphor to be pried open, an ancient goddess that is an anthropological curiosity, a goddess whose marriage is a sociological model and whose behaviour is worthy of psychological analysis. Perhaps she is all of this but she is much more than the sum of those disciplines. Parvati is *chit*, our very being; she is *shakti* or the energy that animates us and the world around us; her presence is a doorway to *ananda* or

109

Kamakshi
20th century
Thanjavur style, Tamil Nadu
Collection: Harsha Dehejia

In this contemporary Thanjavur style painting Kamakshi presides on a golden throne while Sarasvati and Lakshmi are seated at her feet. The gold embossed throne, guarded by two lions, is framed by a golden archway. Kamakshi holds a sugarcane in her left hand and a lotus in her right. With radiant eyes and draped in a regal red sari she has a strong iconic presence superior to the other two goddesses.

bliss; she is the very embodiment of *saundarya* or beauty, not just sensuous but spiritual, a *spandana* or throb of knowledge through which we seek our own self.

Doctrinally, among the Shaivite goddesses, the pride of place goes to Durga and Kali and not to Parvati. Parvati does not have an independent religious standing and gets the attention of devotees only secondarily and sometimes not at all, as some Shaivites prefer to worship Shiva in his aniconic *linga* form. Most Shaivite hymns are chauvinistic and either ignore or give Parvati a second place. However at a popular level most Shiva devotees do recognise her as his consort and will not bypass her in their religious rituals and worship. For that matter, for many devotees she is the doorway to Shiva, and it is she who will intercede on their behalf. This is seen particularly in the Tamil country where Parvati has an independent shrine of her own at all Shiva temples. The most effusive religious sentiment towards Parvati is seen at the annual festival of her marriage to Shiva, which is observed at many Shiva temples, but none so fervently as at the Minakshi-Sundereshavara temple at Madurai. The devout Tamilian believes that witnessing the wedding festival of Minakshi, spread over twelve days, is the greatest event for a pilgrim. Clearly Minakshi asserts her primacy at this wedding festival, observed in the month of *chaitra*, and it is here that the androcentric pattern of sectarian Shaivism is reversed. Myth and ritual part company as Minakshi emerges not only as a goddess of the temple but equally a queen of the city. The daily temple rituals are explicit about Miankshi's ritual precedence and devotees must enter the temple through her doorway and the temple is considered primarily her abode. The four daily rituals at the temple are offered to her first and only then to Shiva. In processions that are a vital part of the wedding celebrations

Minakshi has an independent standing and her image is carried and venerated separately. The ritual practices of the Minakshi temple as well as the wedding festivities are not only an assertion of Minakshi as both goddess and queen at the same time but equally validate the sanctity of the city of Madurai. It is she who expands the sacred space of the temple to the city of Madurai as a whole for it is she who reigns supreme not only in the heart of Shiva's devotees but equally in the secular life of its citizens. And finally, it is because of Minakshi that Vaishnavites and Shaivites, who are not always at peace with each other, come together in a common bond of rejoicing at least for the wedding festival, for after all Shiva is Vishnu's brother-in-law. It is Minakshi who is the common bond between the pre-Aryan Shiva and the Vedic Vishnu and who are characterised by a host of other differences.

The coming together of regality and divinity in Minakshi, where she is not only a goddess but equally a queen and Shiva not only a God but a king, is primarily a product of the *bhakti* movement in Tamil Nadu. This concept of *rajapochara* or looking upon god as king and goddess as queen legitimised many formal practices of temple worship, practices that grew out of the ancient *agamas*. By the same token it was the same concept that granted divinity to a king or queen. This had far-reaching social and political implications in the concept of kingship. The concept of regarding Minakshi as queen as well as goddess, although latent in the Tamil tradition, played an equally important part in the development of the performing arts in South India and was concretised at least since the 10th century. A song or dance that extolled the sensuous beauty of Minakshi eulogised at the same time her divine grace. In this way Minakshi helped bridge the gap between the sacred and the secular in the arts into an integral whole.

If Minakshi is the epitomy of a goddess in the southern *bhakti* and religious tradition, to the aesthete steeped in the tenets of Kashmir Shaivism, she is Parvati *vimarshini*. Kashmir Shaivism is a strongly *advaitic*, non-dualistic, system of philosophy developed around the 10th century and which is subsumed under the generic term Tantra. The Kashmir Shaivite postulates a unique epistemology or system of knowledge from which emerges a world-view that has underpinned Indian aesthetics for the last millennium. In this system, in its barest essence, the core of ultimately reality, whether at the level of *atman*, the microcosm, or *brahman*, the macrocosm, is a pulsating, dynamic *chitananda* or joyous self-awareness, an awareness that includes and does not negate the world around, that affirms and does not reject sensuality, where *maya* or the sensual delights of the world are to be celebrated and not negated as an illusion as it is through it that we ultimately know oursleves. That *chitananda* for the Kashmir Shaivite is what leads the individual from the tentative position of *aham*, "I am" to the initial realisation *aham idam*, "I am myself", and then to the ultimate realisation *aham evam vishvarupam*, "I am the entire world". In Kashmir Shaivism epistemology that *chitananda* is not just an empty, solipsistic, inward, somnolent, passive consciousness or awareness but a dynamic, pulsating, active awareness that is biune or which has two components, which though two are like two as in one, like a couple in sexual bliss or like a word and its meaning. Those two components of awareness are called Shiva and Parvati, Shiva and Shakti, the passive and the active, the male and the female. Parvati is the active energising principle of that awareness also called *shakti* or *vimarshini*. As is said in Kashmir Shaivism parlance *shaktihi shivasysa shivata*, which is to say that the very essence of Shiva is his Shakti. It has also been said that Shiva without his Shakti is a *shava* or a corpse. The dormant, somnolent male or the Shiva component of awareness is energised by the repeated activity by the active, energetic, female or the *shakti* principle and it is only when the two are brought in dynamic harmony that perfect self-realisation is achieved. This in essence is the Kashmir Shaivite position which is in stark contrast to the position taken by Shankara in his system of Advaita Vedanta. The high priest of Kashmir Shaivism was the 10th century philosopher Abhinavagupta and it is this system of philosophy that underpins aesthetic activity and exalts it to a higher level.

An important branch of Kashmir Shaivism is *mantra shastra* or the science of *mantras*. What the cosmic *mantra "aum"* is to Vedantins the *mantra "aham"* is to Kashmir Shaivites, where the sound 'a' stands for Shiva, 'h' for Parvati and 'm' is the *bindu* or the *anusvara*. In chanting *aham* one is not only asserting the togetherness of Shiva and Parvati as *purusha* and *prakriti* but equally realising that it is Parvati who herself brings the chant to a point of stillness through the *bindu*. The *mantra* is a testament to the fact that a proper celebration, cognition and enjoyment of Parvati by Shiva , as in the intonation of the sound 'h', brings Shiva, as in the sound 'a' to that ultimate state of realisation, peace and quietitude as in the sound 'm'.

It is important to sketch out the basic postulates of Kashmir Shaivism as it bears a strong resemblance not only to the narrative of Shiva and Parvati, particularly of their marriage, but equally to its various images. In pointing out this resemblance one cannot posit a causal relationship between the two. The narrative and the images of Parvati obviously evolved independently of Kashmir Shaivism but the resemblance is so strong that it cannot be brushed aside. Knowing one leads to a greater enjoyment and appreciation of the other, and from this

emerges the aesthetic meaning of Parvati. As the narrative of
Parvati stresses, it is she who draws Shiva away from his solitary
and inward meditation, for she knows that Shiva by himself will
not achieve self-realisation. This presumption is the basic tenet of
Kashmir Shaivism, namely that realisation ensues from including
and indulging and not eliminating and withdrawing from the
objective world. While the meditative Shiva is the perfect
cognising subject, the sensuous Parvati is the perfect object, he a
yogi and she a *yogini*. In creating lust in Shiva towards her,
Parvati ensures that Shiva is aroused from his meditative slumber
and that the subject and object come together, just as a romantic
couple are drawn towards each other. Parvati is not only
sensuously beautiful, but is the right object for Shiva's meditation.
Parvati proves herself to be the consummate object, the perfect
companion for Shiva, just as the art object has to be honed to
perfection for the aesthete's delectation. The romantic dalliance
between Shiva and Parvati, when Shiva is not only drawn closer
to Parvati but comes to a perfect understanding of her through
repeated encounters, is akin to the activity of an aesthete who
undertakes an aestheic contemplation of an art object through a
sustained and penetrating study and enjoyment of that object and
not by a cursory glance. The marriage is arranged, Shiva is
committed to Parvati, the aesthete to his art object. The various
activities in Kailasa like making a quilt together, playing dice or
preparing *bhang*, Siva's favourite drink, so charmingly brought out
in the *pahadi* miniature paintings, bring the two closer to each
other and create that bond of affection between the two, just as
the aesthete becomes fonder of the art object by repeated
cognitions. Shiva embraces Parvati romantically and this *alingan*
or embrace is the aesthete's grasping of the art object, a desire to
remain close to it and never be separated from it. The dominant
emotion between Shiva and Parvati at this stage, like that of the

aesthete and the art object, is that of *shringara* or romance, a romance that tarries through the hills and vallies of Kailasa when Shiva identifies himself with Parvati as if saying *aham idam*, "I am this". Shiva and Parvati are now engrossed in each other, even reside in each other, like the two halves of the *ardhanarishvara*. It is interesting to note that even the Nataraja, when he dances his *ananda tandava*, dance of bliss, is in an androgyn state, as evidenced by the left earring which is a *kundala*, a female earring. And at that point the emotion changes, romance is transformed into *adbhuta*, wonder. In coming to know, love and enjoy Parvati Shiva has come to know his own self. It is as if he looks in the mirror that Parvati holds and sees himself in it. In this state of amazement brought about by the mirror of Parvati Shiva is wonderstruck and exclaims "*Shivoham!*" I am Shiva. It is Parvati who has transformed the slumberous Shiva, unaware of his own self, into the joyous, excited and self-realised Shiva. Parvati is not just instrumental but inherent in Shiva's joy and ecstasy. This is the aesthetic meaning of Parvati.

It is clear that the myth of the marriage of Shiva and Parvati, and secondarily the many images of romantic togetherness that it has inspired, are both paradigms of the system of knowledge that Kashmir Shaivism espouses. This is possible because myth is not a mere idle tale but the beautiful expression of a primal reality, a primitive systemof knowledge, and is therefore capable of multiple meanings. For the Kashmir Shaivite Shiva is the consummate aesthete in quest of an aesthetic experience and Parvati the perfect art object and the interaction between the two, the dynamics of an aesthetic experience. For Kashmir Shaivities aesthetic experience was no mere psychological activity but a transcendent experience and *rasananada* or the bliss of such an experience was none other than *brahmananda*, ultimate bliss.

All this yet does not exhaust the meanings of Parvati. Her relationship with Shiva has ontologic significance as well for it reveals the nature of godhead itself. Many are the games that she plays with but in particular her game of dice where Shiva ultimately loses and is destroyed is a paradigm of *lila* or a divine sport and Shiva's defeat in that game an illustration of the ultimate cosmic sacrifice of *purusha*, primal man where the body of a primordial being becomes the raw material from which the cosmos is made.

While the *bhakta*, the devout, and the *rasika*, the aesthete, derive their own learned meanings of Parvati, to the ordinary woman of India Parvati is a friend with whom she can share her mundane world, a sister who understands the complexities of a married woman's life, a trusted confidant with whom she shares her unspoken thoughts. The various folk festivals and household rituals, while lacking in sophistication and not backed by erudite doctrines are an expression and an outlet of those simple feelings of love and affection of an everyday Hindu woman for Parvati and for whom Parvati assumes a sustaining, living reality.

Thus each of us, compelled by our *shiksha* or training, driven by our *drishti* or viewpoint, sustained by our *sanskara* or latent psychic impressions perhaps from a previous birth, derive our own meaning of Parvati. For a brief private moment Parvati belongs to each of us. We celebrate her glory and greatness in our own way. However Parvati cannot be fragmented, her integrity cannot be splintered. Her myth and ritual are parts of the same whole, her songs and stories are lyrics of the same melody, her many images just different streams that flow into the same river, the regional variations in her festivals and rituals leaves of the same *peepal* tree, the stone sculptures and terracotta images arise from the same earth of which she is the goddess of love.

Vidai, Taking Leave

It is customary for an author to reveal the sources from which the book arose and suggest further reading. The sources of my understanding and celebration of Parvati have been the people of India through whose words and rituals, festivals and fairs, Parvati has become a part of my life, a certain Uma who embodies the spirit of Parvati and who once said to me that love should be celebrated for its own sake, the many ancient temples where images of Parvati still whisper to me of her love of Shiva, the magnificent monolithic Kailasa at Ellora where Parvati still roams in the corridors, the many shrines where I rubbed shoulders with the devout as they worshipped and venerated Parvati and found that their faith rubbed off on me, from dancers and musicians who through their gestures and music have brought the many moods of Parvati to life, the scholars whom I met and whose knowledge I richly tapped through my unending questions, the various exhibitions and museums where I found myself touching her feet despite signs that asked me not to and from perusing glossy catalogues where I was pained to see a price tag underneath her image. I commend all of these to you.

I have derived the classical narrative of Parvati from Shiva Purana (Motilal Banarasidass, 1970) The Presence of Shiva (Stella Kramrisch, Princeton University Press, 1981) Hindu Myths (Penguin, edited by Wendy O'Flaherty, 1975), God Inside Out, Siva's Game of Dice (Don Handelman and David Shulman, Oxford University Press, 1997), Tamil Temple Myths (David Dean

Shulman, Princeton University Press, 1980), Sacred Marriage of a Hindu Goddess (William P. Harman, Motilal Banarasidass, 1989). The narrative in the folk tradition is available in vernacular languages. I would recommend Mountain Goddess (William S. Sax, Oxford University Press, 1991) for an excellent account of Nandadevi and Pastoral Deities in Western India (Gunther-Dietz Sontheimer, Oxford University Press, 1993).

To get a flavour of the Tamil bhakti literature I would recommend Slaves of the Lord (Dehejia,V., Munshiram Manoharlal, 1988)

For the literature on Parvati I read Kumarasambhava (Kale, Motilal Banarasidass, 1986), Saundaryalahari (Subramanian, Motilal Banarasidass, 1977), An Anthology of Sanskrit Court Poetry (Daniel H.H. Ingalls, Cambridge University Press, 1965) The many beautiful mediaeval plays and poetry dedicated to Parvati are hard to find except in a very specialised library.

For the images of Parvati I have derived much from the monumental exhibition and its catalogue Manifestations of Shiva (Stella Kramarisch, Philadelphia Museum of Art, 1981).

Finally to those of you who want to taste the joys of Kashmir Shaivism I would recommend Pratyabhijna, The Secret of Self-Recognition (Jaideva Singh, Motilal Banarasidass, 1977). This is an easy to read little book. After this you could try my Parvatidarpana (Dehejia, Motilal Banarasidass, 1997).

Glossary

Abhaya: fearless

Adbhuta: the emotion of amazement or wonder

Adidampati: the primal couple

Advaita: non-dual, usually refers tomonistic systems of philosophy where there is oneness between man and God

Agama: ancient or traditional, the agamas are considered the traditional or prehistoric scriptures of the Indian tradition. Although they accept theauthority of the *Vedas* they exposit a world view different from that of the *nigamas*

Akshamala: rosary of beads

Alingan: embrace

Ananda: bliss

Ankush: goad used for elephants

Ardhanari: ardhangani, a woman whose other half resides in her husband

Artha: meaning

Asura: demon

Atmadarshan: vision or realisation of one's true self

Bhakta: devotee

Bhado: bhadrapad, the months of August and September

Bhang: hemp, an intoxicant, favourite drink of Shiva

Bhanga: deflection on the vertical axis in an image or icon

Bimba: fruit that produces a red juice

Bhikshatana: mendicancy

Chitta: individual mind or consciousness

Chaupat: ancient Indian game played with dice

Chauri: whisk

Chatri: umbrella

Devi: goddess

Dhoti: garment draped around the lower body

Dhvani: reverberation. In Indian semantics it refers to an extended metaphor

Dhyana: contemplation, concentration

Ekantika: single minded

Ektara: one-stringed drone

Gana: attendant of Shiva

Gatha: story

Gopuram: spire of a southern temple

Grahstha: householder

Gramadevi: village goddess

Hamsa: mythic swan that has the capacity to separate milk from water

Hastamudra: hand gesture employed by dancers and used by sculptors for icons

Haveli: mansion

Iti iti: it is this, it is this. In Tantric epistemology it refers to the act of affirmation

Jharokha: balcony of a haveli. In literature and paintings it has romantic connotation

Kalam: pen or genre of painting

Kalasha: ritual pot

Kalpavriksha: wish-fulfilling tree

Kamadhenu: the wish-fulfilling cow

Karandamukuta: tiered conical crown

Katha: story

Katakamudra: gesture depicting the holding of a bracelet

Kinshuka: plant that produces fragrant yellow flowers

Kinnara: mythic creature, half-man and half-animal

Kirtankar: performer who elucidates a doctrine or story through songs and mime

Kundala: earring for a woman

Lalitasana: graceful posture in which one leg is pendant and the her bent at the knees

Lavanga: fragrant spring flower

Lasya: slow movement of dance

Linga: aniconic phallic form of Shiva

Maya: the term carries several meanings. Episematically in Shankara's *Advaita Vedanta* it means the unexplainable illusion of the world appearing as reality. In Kashmir Shaivism however it refers to the power and freedom of the infinite to concretise itself in the finite.

Marukan: son-in-law

Mridanga: type of drum

Mudra: hand gesture used in dance and icons

Mala: garland or rosary

Nakhashikha: the traditional way of describing the beauty of a woman from head to toe

Namarupa: the manifest world of name and form

Navaratra: the festival of the goddess spread over nine nights

Nayika: romantic heroine

Nayikabheda: different types of romantic heroines

Neti neti: not this, not this. In *Vedanta* it refers to the act of negation

Nigama: classical doctrine referring to the Vedic and Upanishadic stream of thought

Odhni: garment draped over the upper body by women, veil, scarf

Pahadi: of the montains. It usually refers to the genre of miniature painting in the Himalayan kingdoms like Guler and Kangra

Pan: betel nut leaf which is a common after-dinner digestive

Parijataka: tree that produces tiny fragrant white flowers with an orange stem. This is one of the trees that is said to grow in Indra's garden

Patua: scroll painting

Prakriti: primal matter, considered female

Pralambana: pendant

Purusha: primal person, considered male

Pradakshina: circumambulation around the sanctum undertaken at the end of worship in a temple

Pratistha: establishment

Pratyabhijna: the Tantric system of knowledge which stresses repeated cognitions

Purana: ancient mythic stories

Raga: melody form adopted in classical music

Rajpopachara: offering made to a king

Rangamandapa: the theatre of the temple

Rasa: artistic expression of emotion

Rasika: an aesthete, a lover of the arts

Rudraksha: beads from a tree sacred to devotees of Shiva and worn around the neck

Sadhana: spriritual endeavour

Sahitya: literature

Sakhi: female friend, love messenger

Samudra manthan: mythic event where the ocean was churned by the gods and the demons

Samyoga: love in union

Sanyasi: male ascetic

Sanyasini: female ascetic

Sanskara: latent psychic impressions from a previous birth

Saundarya: beauty

Shabari: a tribal woman

Shakti: energy. A term usually applied to the consorts of Shiva

Shastra: treatise

Shilpi: artist, sculptor

Shiksha: training or discpline

Shirisha: plant with white flowers

Shringara: emotion of romance

Spandana: vibration, throbbing. A term used in Tantric philosophy

Sthalapurana: local legends associated with a temple

Suchihasta: gesture of pointing

Sundari: beautiful damsel

Tandava: dance of Shiva

Tribhanga: thrice broken pose commonly seen in dancers and icons

Trishul: trident, carried by Shiva and his devotees

Tapasvini: woman who undertakes penance

Tapasya: penance

Utsavmurti: festival icon that is taken out in a procession

Varada: bestowing a boon

Vidyadhara: attendant of Shiva possessing magical powers

Vimarshini: consciousness that affirms and congnises the objective world

Viyoga: seperation

Vyakta avyakta: manifest yet unmanifest

Yajna: a fire sacrifice performed according to Vedic ritual

Yogini: woman who performs yoga

Yojana: eight-mile distance